SHEATHED BAYONETS

& Other Stories

LOUIS PHILLIPS

Published by World Audience, Inc.

©2017, Louis Phillips
ISBN: 978-1541295988

CONTENTS

To the memory of

Bobby Bass

more brother than brother-in-law.

HOW MANY PIECES TO THE DAY?

Fourth Graders were singing:

> *Merrily, merrily, merrily*
> *Life is but a dream.*

Sure it is, kids. Tell it to the 13 year old girl who had been stoned to death as nearly a thousand people stood by and watched in a stadium in the port city of Kismayo, Somalia. The girl had been raped by 3 men in Mogadishu, Somalia, and thus had been accused of adultery by Islamic militants. What were the executioners thinking? How righteous they were? In what reality were they living? Go on singing:

> *Merrily, merrily, merrily,*
> *Life is but a dream.*

How many pieces to the day?

I turned right at the end of an un-mopped corridor and entered Anitra Pullham's office. Anitra Pullham, Ph.D. is our school's principal. My errand is to flirt with the secretary. As everybody in my school district knows, I am in love with the young woman who manages Anitra's office. Such is the way the Cyprian goddess works. Aphrodite is the goddess who creates heart-wrenching realties. As the Chorus in *Hippolytus* sings in the Richmond Lattimore translation:

> *Love distills desire upon the eyes,*
> *Love brings bewitching grace into the heart*
> *Of those he would destroy.*

A Greek tragedy or a Geek tragedy is in the making.

Say not so.

Well, I'd love to hear the 4th Graders sing that Euripidesian ode. It would bring variety to our music program. It would also bring our music program to a screeching halt. Within days, parents would be up in arms, stoning the teachers. If I have to sit through *Row, Row Your Boat* or *Frere Jacques* one more time, I'll shoot myself.

I am surprised the 4th graders aren't singing "Mr. Boyer is in love with Lydia. Mr. Boyer is in love with Lydia." Or perhaps they are saving it for the Christmas concert when my wife will be in attendance. Ames, the Choral director hates my guts, and I wouldn't put such a marriage-ending moment past him.

What God creates such conflicts of the heart?

Lydia—*Love distills desire upon the eye,*—tells me that she has to take her son to the doctor's office. Her son was to meet her at our decaying-infra-structure school, the home of the eternally destitute, but that she just received a phone call from Emmett. He is lost. He is thirteen and on the west side of Manhattan when he should be on the East Side. It is the modern world where a person of any age, complete with a global positioning system, can get lost. My moral compass points in all directions at once. Lost. Oh lost!

Perhaps there is an alternative reality where everything turns out the way it should.

More pieces to the day....

We can, if you so desire, start here with the way reality operates. Or find me another, hence more true, reality if you prefer. Or a school day filled with tender mercies, a day named *tsuris* from the Yiddish meaning trouble or aggravation, from a Semitic root that mean "to become narrow". Trouble narrows us in many ways. Narrows our ability to perceive the waking world. Trouble is a part of life that stands frequently for the entire life. Am I being serious about Souris? Yes, I am. One person morphs, as in dreams, into another. Perhaps life is but a dream. Hamlet on roller-skates. As I return to the auditorium, fourth graders sing in Catalan:

Germà Jaume, Germà Jaume.
Estàs dormint? Estàs dormint?
Sonen les campanes, sonen les campanes.
Ding, dang, dong! Ding, dang, dong!

On etspolze?, On etspolze?
Só caquí. Só caquí.
Gust en saludar-te. Gust en saludar-te.
Jame'nvaig. Jo també.

P.S. 606 is nothing if not an equal opportunity school. As for that sleeping monk, perhaps the song in whatever language it is sung refers to one of the Templar Knights—Frère Jacques de Molay who was executed in 1314.

Executioners are also equal opportunity employers. I don't break step, but quickly walk away from the singing, continuing my review. Ruthie, the school librarian waves at me.

A few fingers at a time. Then she returns to placing newspapers in log-like wooden holders. I have no desire to sleep with her. *Jame'nvaig. Jo també.* I was going sneak a copy of Penne Ahmed's book—*Shipping Semen? How to Have a Successful Experience* – but I think better of it. If I get caught, too many things to explain. Public school teachers already have enough problems to deal with. Poverty for one.

Right outside the library doors is a wastepaper basket in which some disgruntled student has tossed a copy of *Mrs. Pizzlewizzle's Magic.* That's what I need: magic. I need a Magic Day. I drop my book on top of Pizzlewizzle, a perfect pairing. Will give Ruthie something to talk about.

*   *   *

We vacate movie theaters as if awakening from a dream. Who died while we were praising shadows on the wall of a cave? Before going to bed, I watch the final quarter of the Celtics vs. Lakers. Adding to the drama are frequent commercials for a toilet bowl freshener company.

The Celtics win!

The players on the winning team are all smiles and slapping high fives. The losers look glum and think: Why couldn't the Great God of Sports have written a different ending? Is that what we want out of life, a different ending? Alternate universes? Dream languages where no one is stoned to death or left lonely in an empty room?

I alone have escaped to tell thee?

All these are pieces of the same day, so let us try this: We are not strolling on the Via Laietan. By *we* I mean the school secretary and her two young sons Emmett and Timothy. We are walking through a very rich neighborhood in Philadelphia. We are walking down a very straight and narrow street, bounded on one side by magnificent houses. We four are in Philadelphia because Lydia's husband has flown off to the Basque region of Spain for a conference, and because the Phillies won the World Series.

The street is bounded on the west side by cattails.

All the white houses have doors of oak or mahogany. Antique garden statuary dot the well-mown lawns. One house proudly displays a blackamoor torchese. Grottoes have been imported from Spain. Catalan. Houses are flanked by Roman temples, so an architectural student might label many of the houses as Capriccios.

But as we start back from wherever we came from—Franklin Park or PS 660—I realize we are lost. In spite of the fact that the street is perfectly straight and narrow, I cannot get us to where we need to be. Lydia has to go to the bathroom, and is even willing to usea Porto-san, but I don't believe they are clean enough, so I locate a clean restroom at a gas station that is built like a large white house.

The drive-way near the gas pumps is covered with oil-slicks, on the ground lay newspapers which are in wooden log-like library holders.

When Lydia goes to the bathroom, her sons remove the newspapers from the holders and use them as canes, and then as swords.

While Emmett and Timothy are fooling around, I approach a man who is standing in front of his white SUV. From over his left shoulder I see a woman whom I assume is his wife. His wife isnear tears. I ask, "Do you know the way back to the Holiday Inn near Franklin Park?"

He says. "I cannot help you. Everything I have has been stolen from my van."

I murmur my condolences in a language I myself do not understand. Probably Basque. Possibly English. More than likely the language of dreams. Who does not speak that language?

4

Back at the Holiday Inn, the boys have their own room and Lydia and I have an adjacent one. We lie naked in the bed, but she won't allow me to fuck her. It's her period. We lie spoons and I hold her swollen breasts.

5

In the faculty section of the school cafeteria, Herbert Taubman is seated at a table all by himself. He reads a book and from time to time his right hand snakes its way into a paper bag and pulls forth something green.

I decide to ruin his lunch.

"All right if I sit with you?' I ask, knowing how much he despises me. He believes I may have been too friendly with his wife, a woman from Korea.

He grunts. I sit.

Herbert is in his mid-fifties and his hair is already white. His face bears the scars left from a severe bout of small pox, and he speaks as much through his nose as he does his mouth.

"What are you reading?" I believe I recognize the book.

"*Shipping Semen? How to Have a Successful Experience*," he says, flashing the cover of the book so I can see that he's not making up the title."

"Sounds good I say." I fish a tuna fish sandwich on whole wheat bread out of my bag. One of the saddest things in my small world: I am a grown man still brown-bagging my lunch to school just as I did when I was in first grade. Probably the same sandwich in the same bag. Certainly not the same boy.

At least I hope not. It's not easy to tell being inside of one consciousness only, viewing the world from inside out.

I think that if just once had a dream, and if I could piece together where all the parts of the dream came from that I would stand at the threshold of decoding the string theories that explains our universe.

Unfortunately with dreams, they take too much work to understand fully. Too many moving parts. "Why are you reading a book like that?" I ask, needling him a bit more. Not that he needs needling from me. He has twogrown kids and his daughter is driving him crazy. Couldn't happen to a nicer guy.

"I'm not reading it," he says sharply.

"Oh. I thought you were."

"I fished it out of the trash before one of the children got is hands on it. What kind of idiot brings a book like that to school? If a child took it out of the wastepaper basket and brought it home, do you know what kind of hell would break out?"

"Don't worry, Herb. Nobody from our school ever brings a book home."

"You always have a wisecrack, don't you?"

"Not always." I guess he's right. I should never have brought that book to school. Dumb. Dumb. My brain has become the museum of weird. The Museum of Morbid Anatomy has closed.

He closes the book and stuffs it into his briefcase. I believe he grows mushrooms in there. "You and your Commie-Socialist ideas."

I stand up and take my lunch bag to the trash receptacle. WhenI leave I see Herbert seated where I left him, forlornly playing with a red rubber band. Tomorrow he is going to be one of the chaperones on the school trip. I am pleased I am not going along. The school will be much more quiet.

6

Doot-in doo-doo, feeling Groovy.

O the World, with its pipes & whines and labyrinths of Muzak spilling out the guts of Simon and Garfield singing. Tuesday morning. June l7th. The school year, at last, winding down.

Herbert Taubman, who wasn't feeling Groovy or even groovy, paid for his breakfast, tipped the waitress, walked a block to catch the bus to middle school 197 where he served *(served time, as in a prisoner?)* as the Assistant Principal. It was easy to walk to the bus stop. He only had to follow the straight line of the sidewalk. Not like the twists and turns of thoughts that came upon him from God knows where. Basic mean thoughts.Basic suicide thoughts. Basic envy thoughts.

At age 55.he thought. I am running out of time. As soon as I get up to start the day I am tired, but that's the way of the world. Not the play by Congreve where Betty the maid says if the clock that is always pushing us forward. "Turned the last canonical hour." It's merely the way of the waking world with allthe 10,000 or so pieces of each day, with all its labyrinths. How easy to find our way in; how difficult to find our way back.

7

"The Labyrinth is one of the oldest of symbols; it depicts the way to the unknown center, the mystery of death and rebirth."

—Edward Whitmont, *The Return of the Goddess (1972).*

Maybe by having my body frozen, I could return to existence at some later date. Ask Danny, he thought. That was Danny Robb's field of interest. He was cold enough to embody it. Danny's nephew, age 8, had died of diabetes in a Germantown nursing home, and now his sister and her husband were being held responsible for their child's death because they had refused, because they are Christian Scientist, to administer, as their doctor had advised them, insulin. Why have children, Herbert thought, if you cannot protect them from harm?

Mortality in a groove.

On the bus a woman and young man at Herbert's right were discussing surfing: "I lived on the beach and used to go surfing at lunch time. Of course, the waves at

Dia were small and not very exciting, but it was still relaxing. Nothing better than surfing."

The man seated to Herbert's left weighed 600 lbs. and wore a black t-shirt with a photo of Hank Williams on it. The shirt also weighed 600 pounds. No wonder the Assistant Principal had to stand. The fat man asked him, "Do you know Sylvester?"

"The cat?"

"Yeah."

"With Tweety Bird."

"Yeah. Well, I have this t-shirt at home and just show the Sylvester the pussy cat and the word *Whipped* under it. Get it?"

Herbert got it.

The 600 pound Hank Williams' fan was speaking too loudly for me to be comfortable standing next to him. "I mean he's a kind of a cat. Get it?"

"I get it." If he had been younger, he would have gotten off the bus and walked.

"And he stands with his paws turned down. Get it?"

The bus was air-conditioned, but the fat clown was sweating. He could drown in his own sweat. Wishful thinking on Herbert's part.

"I mean I thought it was so funny. I couldn't stop laughing.

There was a whole stack of these T-shirts, selling for $5.00. I should of bought them all. I mean it was so funny."

Herbert, who did not find it funny at all, nodded and returned his attention to the surfers.

"Hey," the man called, pulling on the sleeve of Herbert's coat. "Do you know how deep the generations of Hank Williams go? I mean he had a son, and that son had a son. Do you know if that son had a son?"

The bus stopped one block before my school, and Herbert got off. He realized Danny would be soon making the trip to Philadelphia to act as a character witness on his sister's behalf.

Three yellow school buses from a company in Yonkers were waiting patiently. They were to take the seventh graders to Ocean Wonder Park. Herbert would have rather eaten a plate of dead frogs than accompany a bus-load of screaming, hormone-loaded adolescents anywhere, let alone to an amusement park. He could feel his temples throbbing. And it was not even nine o'clock.

Charles Darwin, Elvis Presley, Thomas Jefferson and Herbert. They all suffered from migraines. Better to vomit dead frogs. He adjusted his leather broad-brimmed hat. Keep the sun off. Keep the sun off. Photons carry information. So do humans but they are impossible to comprehend.

Give me a sub-atomic particle any day, Herbert thought.

8

The street that led to Intermediate School 197 was not Easy Street. Anyone could tell you that. And Herbert's thoughts were marching to some calithumpian band. For some reason, Herbert started thinking about his grandmother and the first and, perhaps, the only taxi-cab ride she ever took in her life. And then the deep water into which he peered and saw all manner of creatures. Sea Turtles and snakes and crocodiles. And he had lost his shoe and the shoe had dropped into the cold water.

Herbert's grandmother had gone down town and couldn't get a bus in time, so she took a cab to the house of Herbert's parents.

Thump thump thump went the big bass drum of the calithumpian band that accompanied thoughts that marched in from out of nowhere. Thoughts, like photons, seemed to be in different places at the same time.Someone under the water had recovered Herbert's shoe and placed the shoe into a basket to be pulled up by ropes and pulleys. Not only the shoe, however. When the cab arrived, Nana paid the fare and tipped the driver a nickel. Herbert hated to repeat what the driver said to his grandmother. Yes, he would hate to repeat it. *Thump. Thump. Thump.* Groovy.

Inside the basket with the black shoe, the underwater person had placed a huge sea turtle. When Herbert had hauled up the basket, he had to lift out the turtle and then take out the shoe. Persons who were watching laughed. Herbert felt good because he had made others feel good.

When God laughed, millions of people died.

On the corner of the school, a wire trash basket was smoking. Herbert stopped, and looked inside trying to find any liquid that might prevent a fire. It was then he noticed a fire-truck just a few feet away. In his two black shoes, size 1l, Herbert, filled with confidence, walked to the truck.

One of the firemen was leaning out the window and Herbert tapped him on the arm. "Did you guys come to put out that fire?" Herbert asked, pointing toward the smoking trash basket.

The fireman said something to his partner and they got down from the truck.

Why, Herbert thought, should I try to find something to put out the fire when the firemen were already there, but as he walked away, heading for the yellow busses, he felt guilty? Suppose they thought he had started the fire. Suppose they called him back for questioning? He quickened his pace, walking away from the truck, the fire, his dead grandmother, and his last night's dream. If he could only walk away from the pains in his head, the thumping, the careless thoughts that go nowhere, but round and round and come out here. To the men studying the smoldering wire basket, Herbert sang softly from the Grateful Dead, "*Keep on truckin'—like the Doodah Man.*" Some days there was nothing to rely upon but music.

9

By nine, three bus-loads of seventh graders, each bus accompanied by three teachers, started the trek to New Jersey. The bus Herbert was on contained, in addition to four teachers, the head of the phys-ed department, the assistant principal (Herbert) and a nurse. Yes, Herbert thought, this is what education has come to. No History, English, or Math. Just keep the little bastards amused. Keep parents appeased by passing their children up the ladder to early pregnancies, early marriages and early brain-numbing jobs, as if their brains were not numb all ready. Their lives were over before they even got a chance to start them.

Like waking up tired.

I am tired before I begin, Herbert thought. All I do all day is put out fires. One problem stomped on, then a new one crops up.

∗   ∗   ∗

The Game Boys and whatever electronics that had been bought, begged, stolen, were out in full regalia. Only a few teachers and one or two students had cell phones. But it did not take a genius to predict that it was only a matter of time before everyone would have phones in their hands all hours of the day and night. The Future was already behind us.

The new generation had a lower threshold of boredom of any previous generation. O dear, embodying the consciousness of the gods, let us go. The Minotaur is waiting for its daily quota of human sacrifice, Baal or Lord.

Herbert took a seat next to Sally Hitchcock, the 7th Grade English teacher and past chair of the English Dept. Herbert and Sally had been colleagues then friends for more than 20 years. She and Herbert were now both in their mid-fifties, both married, both putting on weight, both showing generous heads of white hair. They had been in the trenches together and had fought many battles with the New York City School Board, with its 400 circles of bureaucratic hell surrounded by swamps of attendant idiocies that sucked the air out of any semblance of joy from teaching. Sally was the only person inside the school that Herbert confided in, shared his personal life with. Whatever personal life he had left. He had never really warmed to Anitra, the principal, but he did not dislike her.

Nor did he disapprove of her.

Noise inside the bus began to rise and Herbert shouted them down. "If I take down your name for misbehaving," he warned them, "then you will stay on the bus with me while your friends are having fun in the pool." It was a hollow threat at best and the students knew it. There was no way he was going to ruin his day by staying on some sneaker-smelling bus. He had brought a good book to read. One where evil is eventually, through pains-taking police procedures, brought to Justice with a capital J. Fiction. Pure fiction.

"How's your daughter doing?" Sally asked. She pulled student themes from a folder. Sally was always very efficient and had decided to use the travel time to get some work done. Multi-tasking. The handwritten themes looked as if a flock of inebriated chickens had walked between the lines.

There was no way that the world, with its immense cosmic reasons to go on living, could depend upon this new generation to save it.

In the beginning, God said, let there be Attention Deficit Disorder. And it was so.

Herbert's daughter Anya had gone off to Wesleyan to begin her first year of college. The bills were killing him. And to top it off, Anya had developed an eating problem and had to be brought home before she starved herself to death.

"She's screaming," Herbert said, staring straight ahead, keeping a close eye on the Puerto Rican bus driver.

"Screaming."

"Yes. Right out of nowhere, right in the middle of doing some exercises or while she is seated at the table, Anya'll just start screaming at the top of her lungs. It takes a long time to calm her down."

"That's terrible.

"We've already been warned by the co-op board. We're going to be thrown out if it doesn't stop."

"She's seeing a therapist, of course."

"Of course, but nothing is getting better. I thought her mother could handle it, but she can't."

Sally tossed back her blonde hair and fastened it with a thick rubber band. Herbert could sense her disapproval of his attitude. Why have children, she was probably thinking, if you cannot protect them from harm?

He was always shoveling domestic problems onto his wife.

"We've been house hunting, but if I like a place, my wife doesn't. And if she likes a place, I don't." Herbert located a rubber band in the pocket of his sport jacket and started playing with it, stretching it over his fingers.

"Take my advice, Herbert," Sally said, "This time she was sympathetic. If your wife likes a place, take it. You'll be happier if she's happy."

"Happy," he repeated. "Who can afford happiness? I'd settle for a little peace and quiet."

Before the bus had crossed the Washington Bridge, Sally had held up a single, slightly crumbled, blue-lined page covered with penciled chicken feet. She laughed.

"What's so funny," Herbert asked. He had been worrying about his daughter.

"This reading report," Sally said. "From Jonas. I had just read an interview with an author who was talking a bout his teaching experiences. How many book reports on *KonTiki* can you read?" She placed the crumpled page on top of the folder and tried to smooth it out. "And look what I get. A book report on *Kon Tiki.*"

"*KonTiki*? Believe me," Herbert said, staring at the seventh-grader in a faded pink t-shirt who was seated five seats ahead, with two of his close friends. Right behind the bus driver. They were sharing a Gameboy. "There is no way Jonas read *KonTiki.*"

"I know," Sally said, "I called him on it. I asked him why come he chose *KonTiki* to read? He said because it was the only book his father had. I guess there are no other books in his house."

Herbert shook his head in sympathy. Boogie Angel and Donald Dean had started punching each other in the arm, until the history teacher put a stop to it. The school bus sighed its way into New Jersey. Dorothy Calabese, the music teacher had stood up, clapped her hands, and tried to get everybody singing Stephen Foster songs, Herbert scowled. Who wanted to sing Stephen Foster? It was a joke and would dissolve into a fiasco, but Ms. Calabese was young, fresh out of college, and enthusiastic. Maybe she could do the impossible. She was already doing the impossible, living on a teacher's salary in Manhattan and commuting to the Bronx every morning.

> *De Camptown ladies sing dis song*
> *CHORUS: Doo-dah! doo-dah!*
> *De Camptown race-track fives miles long--*
> *CHORUS: Oh! doo-dah day!*

After the third chorus, Sally stopped singing. "What do you think of our new Cantor," Sally asked. "Doesn't he have a beautiful voice?"

"Yes," Herbert said, "but there is no sweetness in it. His voice lacks sweetness. The boy who sang after him. Well, his voice was not as strong, but his voice has sweetness, I prefer sweetness."

"Did you ever hear Jonas sing?" Sally asked, circling with red ink spelling error after spelling error. *Volunteer* became for Jonas *val entire*.

"No. Why?"

"Because he has a beautiful singing voice. You might say it has sweetness in it."

"How come he's not in the chorus?"

"Most days he has to go home to look after his four year old brother."

"That's too bad," Herbert said. He rubbed both temples vigorously. Emily Dickinson and Lewis Carroll. For all Herbert knew maybe Lassie suffered from headaches.

"Yes," Sally said, "Yes, it is."

10

It was nearly eleven A.M. by the time the three busses disgorged screaming seventh graders, with their towels a bathing suits, and brown bag lunches, into the awakening of summer. The chaperones tried to impress upon the youngsters the need for sunscreen, the need to form a buddy system to help keep everybody safe, the need to be at the entrance of the Water Park at 4:00 for the return trip home.

As soon as the pupils had eaten lunch and had changed into bathing suits and had placed their clothing into lockers, the classes fanned out for various rides, including the long water slide into a tidal pool.

Sally found a bench in the shade and worked upon her folder of papers. Danny Robb, who was writing a book about cryogenics, and who had told him about Benjamin Franklin's wish, "I wish it were possible…to invent a method of embalming drowned persons in such a manner that they may be recalled to life at any period, however distant"—had brought his 12 year old adopted daughter to the park and he would be spending much of his time watching Noriko.

Herbert walked toward a food stand. Out of the corner of his eye, he saw Jonas, who stood just slightly over five feet, running with Boogie and Donald toward Wildwater Kingdom. Oh! To be young again? No, Herbert thought. One childhood was enough. His own son, Mark, at sixteen and fighting acne was miserable enough. Thank God, he thought, while standing in line, and admiring the blue sky—one thing he would miss after his death would be the sweet blue sky—Thank God, he repeated to himself, the weather was good. A rainy day would have been more than any of them could bear.

CHORUS: Doo-dah! doo-dah!
Dey fly de track and dey both cut across—

For so many children brought here by the school this would be their only visit to a park. For many of them it would be the highlight of their summer, not counting their release from the prison they called school. The teachers would accompany the children on the rides or they would go their own way. Freedom. Glorious freedom to beat up one another.

11

At 20 to four, Herbert stood outside the entrance of the Water Park to make certain the busses were in their place. If the ride down was tempered by anticipation, the ride back would be far more difficult.

The children and teachers would be tired and there would, as usual, be disappointments to be dealt with – rides not ridden, snacks too expensive to enjoy, sunburns, quarrels, indigestion, motion sickness, bruises, the residue of a day's outing facing a long ride back to places not nearly as exciting as the place they were leaving behind.

Large signs posted at the park's main entrance read:

THE WAVE POOL IS FOR STRONG SWIMMERS. LIFE JACKETS SHOULD BE WORN AND ARE PROVIDED FREE OF CHARGE.

By four P.M, the children and their chaperones assembled. Roll was called. Everyone present and accounted for.Every one except one.

"Where's Jonas? Sally asked. "Has anyone here seen Jonas?"

Some mumbling. No response. The head count was taken. Boogie," Herbert called.

"I'm here," Boogie said. He was thin as a needle and was now wearing only his shorts over his bathing suit and sneakers without socks. His black T-shirt was tied about his waist.

"Put your shirt on, Boogie," Herbert told him. "Nobody gets on the bus without wearing a shirt."

Boogie untied his T-shirt and pulled it on.

"Donald."

"I'm here too." A few students laughed. All looked bored. Just standing around.

"Where's Jonas?" Herbert asked. He removed his glasses and pinched the top if his nose. He could feel his heart pounding. This was one thing he always hated about class trips. One kid who gets lost or forgets the time.

The two black boys looked at their feet. Donald shrugged.

Boogie shook his head.

"You just can't go off and leave your friend. Where did you see him last?"

"We didn't do nothing," Booger said.

"I didn't say that. Just tell me where you saw him last.

How long ago since you saw him? Look, come over here and we can talk in private."

"Anybody see Jonas in the last half hour?" the singing teacher asked.

Danny Robb and his daughter stood by themselves off to one side. All of Danny and Sally's students were accounted for. Noriko was licking an ice-cream cone. Soft vanilla. It was melting over her hands. Girls chatted among themselves. Boys tossed a small football and a wet tennis ball. Herbert led the two black boys away from the busses.

"Tell me where you last saw Jonas. Were you in the wave pool with him?"

The two boys started talking together. All three of them had been in the pool and they ended up in the deep end. They admitted Jonas was scared because he had told Boogie that he wasn't a very good swimmer. Waves started crashing into the boys, and Jonas lost his footing and slipped under the water.

"We tried to help him, but he couldn't hold on to him because he was too slippery."

"What happened then?"

"We couldn't see him," Donald said, waving his hands back and forth excitingly. "We dived under but we couldn't see him."

"He slipped too far down," Boogie said,

Herbert held his composure, He didn't want to frighten the two boys more than they were frightened, nor the students and teachers staring in their direction. Everybody was trying to figure out what was happening. Mostly, everybody wanted to go home.

"Where were the lifeguards?" Herbert asked.

"We kept calling to the lifeguards for help, but they didn't come into the pool."

"Why not?"

"We don't know," Boogie said.

"We don't know," Donald repeated.

"You sure you called for the lifeguards."

"We're sure," Boogie said, speaking for them both.

"Maybe they didn't hear you."

"What about your teachers? Weren't there any teachers in the wave pool?"

"No, Sir."

"Did either of you get out of the pool and go to the lifeguards?"

"Yes, Sir."

"Well?"

"The lifeguard said that they saw Jonas getting out of the pool. They said they saw him leave the pool."

"If Jonas left the pool, where is he?"

"We don't know," Boogie said, speaking for the both of them. Donald was on the verge if crying. Herbert put his arms around the boys. "Maybe he did get out of the pool without you seeing him," Herbert told them, not believing what he was saying. "You guys did the right thing. Don't you worry about it. I'll go back and find him." With his arms around the boys, he led them back to their group.

He told the students to get onto the busses, and as the students got on, Herbert gathered the teachers together and told them what had happened.

"I'll go back and find him."

"Shall we have one of the busses wait?" Dorothy asked.

"No. The kids have to get back or the parents will be frantic. I have a friend who lives a few miles away from here. I'll call him and he can pick me up, get me to a train station. Or, if worse comes to worse, I'll call for a cab and charge it to the school." Just follow the straight line back.

"I'll stay with you," Sally volunteered. "Two looking for Jonas will be better than one."

"All right, but somebody will be waiting for Jonas. Dorothy, you'll have to tell them Jonas missed the bus and we'll bring him home later. Tell them to go home and wait for me to call them. When you get to the school see if you can get me the contact information. Call Security and give me Jonas's phone number. That's in case we can't find him. As it is, the buses are going to be very late. Does any one have a cell phone to call the school? The guard there can alert the parents."

"I have one," Danny said.

"Good. Just call the school and tell them the busses aregoing to be late."

"What about Jonas? " Danny asked. "Should I say anything about Jonas?"

"No. There's nothing to tell yet. See if you can reach Edith. Our principal has to be alerted."

"What about the police? Should we call the police?"

Herbert sighed and rubbed his forehead. "He hasn't missing that long has he? Just get everybody home safely. Besides, didn't the lifeguards say they saw Jonas leave the pool?" How could they say that? How would they even know Jonas? Did they talk to Jonas at any point? Weren't there some teachers watching the kids? I should have stayed in the wave pool.

12

First stop was the park's security office. There Herbert and Sally told them that Jonas was missing, gave the staff a description.

"Are the life-guards who were on duty at the Wave Pool still on duty?" Sally asked.

The security officer placed a manila file folder on his desk. It contained a list of school trips scheduled for that day and other special visitors. "Did you bring a folder with all the parental release forms, signed, a list of the students with emergency contact information? A photo every student? That's good information to have on hand."

"The release forms are back at the school on the principal's desk," Sally said.

The security officer shook his head. "Good place for it."

"The list of the students—well that went with the teachers on the bus."

"Good place for it," the officer repeated with the same timbre of accusation in his voice.

"What about the life-guards?"

"That we don't know. You have to go to the Manager's office for that." He pointed out the appropriate office. Sally headed there.

First stop for Herbert was the changing room where the boys had changed into their bathing suits or stored their clothes in lockers. The school had commandeered 3 rows of lockers for the boys and one for the male teachers. The lockers were open. Teachers had brought extra padlocks in case a student had forgotten one.

At the bottom of one of the lockers, in a small wire basket, were the clothes Jonas had been wearing: a faded pink T-shirt, black denim cut-offs, sneakers. Well, there was one sneaker.

Why would there just be one sneaker? What would be the sense of that? Of course, it was not unusual for the kids to take one another's clothes as a prank. That was one more reason for the teachers to keep the padlock keys and keep control of the lockers.

The lifeguards who had been at the wave pool, which manufactured 3 foot high waves every 6 minutes, had already gone home for the day, but Frank Ponder, the Park's Managing Director, told Sally that they would be returning that evening with 70 other lifeguards from all over the state to be a part of training exercises.

"Call them at home. Call them. There's a boy's life at stake," The Director scowled. He stared at Sally as if to say she was being too melodramatic, but he went down his phone list and called. The college student named Jeremy answered and, after a few questions, told Frank that he and the other two guards on duty saw the young boy climbing out of the pool and leaving the area." After Frank relayed the information, Sally asked, "Did he describe the boy whom he saw leaving the pool. How could he be sure it was Jonas?"

"I didn't ask him that," said the Director, "but we take every precaution. Our lifeguards are among the best in the state. That's why the State sends so many people here for training."

"So they never turned off the machine that makes the waves?"

"It's not the duty of the life-guards to turn off the machines.

Security does it after we are certain everyone is out of thepark. Also today we had lifeguard training."

"You need to send people back to the pool and drag the pool again. Where else could he be?"

"We got almost 200 acres of amusements, with 38 acres devoted to swimming activities. He could be anywhere, goofing off. We got 30 water rides. Maybe he wanted to try them all. We've checked all the pools. There is no childin any of them. Maybe he just decided to run away."

"Not in his bathing suit."

13

Damn Dorothy! Herbert thought. Here I am walking around a water park searching for a lost child. If I can't find Jonas, going home would be no fun. Not that it would be any fun anyway because of Anya. Any minute she might stand up and start screaming.

Herbert had a friend, about the same age, 55 going on 102, who claimed he had never been depressed. Been lonely, been sad, been angry, been confused, but never depressed which Herbert saw as a combination of loneliness, anger, confusion, sadness, topped with despair. Did not Anya ask him late one night if he would help put her to death? How could a daughter ask that of her father? How could parents live with such knowledge. And what about Jonas's parents? He didn't know anything about Jonas's home life. Were his parents living together? Were they divorced?

There they were, if they were both alive, or there somebody was—a grandparent or aunt—waiting for Jonas to come home and when the busses arrived, there would be no Jonas.

We struggle through the day thinking nothing can go wrong, because if we thought otherwise we would be better prepared. But how can anybody be prepared for so many possibilities.

But at least Herbert had located Jonas's missing sneaker. It had been tossed into the teachers' locker. Someone was playing a joke, a joke that Jonas was still not aware of. A joke that nobody would laugh at. But the fact that Jonas had not returned to change out of his wet bathing suit meant something. But what?

14

From the wave pool to the Bonzai Water Slide to the security building.

It was a circular argument made straight. Or straight argument made circular. It was back and forth. The whirlpool. The avalanche. The Scylla and Charydis. Whatever sucks a person down. Even so, most climb out and walk round and round.

*　　*　　*

The lifeguards came to practice their drills in various pools. Sally and Herbert questioned the three teens who had been on duty at the wave pool.

They insisted they saw the boy pull himself out of the pool and walk off while his friends rough-housed in the water. They swore they heard the boys calling the boy by the name Jonas.

"Could it have been Jonah? One of the seventh graders on the trip was Jonah Westworh."

The lifeguards looked at each other. One said, "Possible."

"What color bathing suit?"

They couldn't answer.

Had they turned off the machine that made the waves?

No. That was Security's job. Besides, it was not clear which swimming pools were going to be used that evening for the training exercises.

After the life-guard drills were held around the Water Park, but no one reported seeing anyone or thing in the water. Round and round it goes, and where life stops nobody knows. If the universe can bounce back like a rubber band, why not the life of a young child?

And what were Jonas's relatives going through. They had called the park, but that was when Sally and Herbert were away from the security office, making separate rounds. It was a phone call that Herbert did not wish to respond to.

The State police arrived and Sally and Herbert faced another round of questioning.

By eleven, Sally and Herbert decided to return to the city and face Jonas's parents. But to tell them what? We started out with a bus load of students and one did not return. What would the relatives say? "You people were out having fun and letting my child drown?"

But, of course, there was no proof of drowning. There was no proof of anything.

"What kind of people are you?"

And did we have enough teachers with us to make certain the students were adequately protected? The thought crossed his head once again: I should have stayed in the Wave Pool.

Herbert tried to reach his friend who lived near the water park, but his friend did not pick up the phone. Sally and Herbert got a ride from Frank Ponder to the train station. It was the least they could do, Herbert thought. The very least they could do. The car radio station was set to Country and Western, and songs would have blared the entire way if Sally had not insisted that he turn it off. It was then Herbert wondered what happened to the stack of student themes she had been grading on the trip down.

They arrived back in the Bronx by 10:30.

At 2 A.M. the phone rang. It was the principal. Her voice was shaky and quavering. This was going to be bad trouble. Was there any such thing as good trouble? "I just got a call from the park," Edith said. Herbert could tell she was near tears. Herbert's wife, frightened by such a late night call, had leapt from their bed to rush to Anya's room. She was afraid that if the phone had awakened Anya, the girl would start screaming.

"They found Jonas's body."

"Where?"

"The wave pool."

"How is it possible?"

"He was wedged into the grating at the deepest end of the pool."

"Who found him?"

"A welder. He had been hired to check on the various tidal gates."

"When was he found?"

"About an hour ago. I just got the call and now I'm calling you."

"What about Jonas's family."

"The police have told them. The grandparents and a younger brother are on the way to Allentown to identify the body."

"Allentown? In Pennsylvania?"

"Don't ask me. That's where they took the body."

"I'm getting dressed. I'll meet you at the school."

"Yes. We need to decide what to do."

Herbert agreed. He hung up the receiver and searched for his shoes. He located one. The second he found in the living room. Thank God Anya had not awakened.

Yes, he thought, tying his laces, they needed to decide what to do.

15

Quietly, I find out from Lydia about the drowned student. Anitrais pulling together a special assembly to tell the students what has happened. Lydia and I commiserate with each other for a few minutes, but truth to be told there is very little to be said. Lydia says that the student was being raised by his grandparents. She did not know what happened to the parents.

So many things happen to other people. There is no way to takekeep track of them all. What we do know is that soon the newspapers will be filled to the brim with attacks upon the school. The school was at fault of course. What a stupid idea to take seventh graders to a water park. Probably better to keep everybody under lock and key. Lawyers are probably lined up around the block, salivating, fighting one another to get the case. A lot of money at stake. It's an ill wind that does not blow somebody some good.

I carry my brown bag of a lunch up to the teacher's lounge, but the lounge is deserted. Eerily so. A desert within a desert. No oasis in sight. Merely a collection of mirages. A collection of phantoms. The assembly would be starting soon enough, and the teachers who acted as chaperons to the park were meeting with the student's grandparents and the police and God knows who else. I felt sorry for them all.

But better the accident happened to other people and not on my watch. Watching how others deal with Fate or Disaster or a bad left turn at Albuquerque is a major form of entertainment. Or distraction. Unless it happens to ourselves. Surprise. Surprise.

Doodah. Man who led police on a high speed chase kills himselfoutside Philadelphia. If it bleeds, it leads. Why was the student's body taken all the way to Allentown? Possibly for an autopsy?

And poor Herbert. I guess he's with the grandparents and perhaps that's the reason he wasn't around to help Anitra with the assembly. Even if I do not like the guy, he's got enough on his plate to deal with. But then again, who doesn't? The jars of the day get filled up with errands. I would never chaperone a class trip. Too many things go wrong.

The door opens and there is Johnny Johnson the elderly Janitor. Alliteration everywhere. Wearing a tan baseball cap, and a black T-Shirt that says, "We were having a dandy time until someone divided by zero." He had told me it was a gift from one of his grandchildren. He said he didn't even know what it meant.

God divides by zero all the time, but I didn't say that.

"Just checking on things," he said. "You all right, Mr. Boyer?"

"Fine, Johnny. I am getting ready to go to the auditorium, so you can sweep in here if you want."

"Thank you." He pushes the industrial broom through the door. "Terrible tragedy," he says.

"Yes. A terrible tragedy," I agree.

"Jonas was a sweet boy."

"I didn't know him," I said. "Maybe he would have been in my eighth grade class." I toss my uneaten lunch into the wastepaper basket. Enough tuna fish. Enough of everything. Enough, enough. Everything in the waste paper basket.

"Good shot," he says, smiling, showing a few gold teeth. It feels as if he has been a janitor for the school for a thousand years. "You ever a basketball player?" He asks, smiling. Teasing me, I guess.

"No. Just watch it on television. These days I get most of my life from television."

"Ain't that the truth? The morning news was all about the missing boy. Had shots of our school and all."

Enough.

"See you later, Johnny."

"Yes, Sir."

As I go out the door, the old saying comes out of nowhere: To err is human. To forgive is divine. But it is most like more true that to err is godlike; to forgive is human.

Our minds of museums of dead thoughts walking. Zombies.

As I go down the stairs, the hallways are filled with teachers, students, parents, school board members, security persons, reporters, all walking with an eerie silence to be assembled. No music today. Life is but a fleeting dream floating over our heads. I remember the words from the Greek Tragedy I had been reading:

Love brings bewitching grace into the heart
Of those he would destroy.

No more music for now.

WHAT?

This is what the bartender said: When I was growing up inCleveland, some of my friends and myself broke into a freight car and you know what?

What?

It was loaded with funeral shrouds. And you know what?

What?

Lots of Kid films: THE KARATE KID. THE KID FROM BROOKLYN.THE KID FROM SPAIN. KID GALAHAD. Wambaugh drew circles on the bar with the wet spot left behind by his beer mug.

These funeral shrouds were so well made that my buddies were able to palm them off as evening gowns. Harry Wambaugh who sat somewhere else could only shake his head. What? At five o'clock in the afternoon what kind of woman brings a four-year-old to the bar with her.Perhaps she was waiting for the free snacks. A freight car loaded with chicken wings. Chicken wings in shrouds.

"Come on, I'm not that drunk." the woman with the three-year-old daughter said. "Or that stupid." She sat on one bar stool; her red-haired daughter in gray sweat pants and a light blue spring jacket sat on another. "Do I look that stupid to you?" Yes, you do, you stupid bitch. The child sipped ginger ale through a straw. On Wednesdays Wellman's Bar and Grill put out fried "I'm not kidding you," the Bartender said, "chicken wings."

There were lots of things a man could do. Designer shrouds for yuppie corpses. Or beer coasters with photographs on them. Personalized beer coasters. Perhaps it would be possible in theory to put together enough to make a satisfying supper of chicken wings. In theory. In practice it wouldn't work out that way.

The child pulled out her straw and allowed drops of ginger ale to dribble on her sweat pants. The woman was in red slacks and a tight green sweater. Kid Millions. The heartbreak kid.It is good to have a hobby. Wambuagh's step-father was a soft-spoken sixty-year-old gent working his way through night school. Why don't you know go back to school, Wambaugh? Because they don't teach me what I want to know. What is it that you want to know? I don't know, but whatever they teach I don't want to know it. She looked like a stoplight in red and green like that. Maybe he would get lucky Wambaugh thought and would get his hands on her stoplights, certainly ample and not bad to think about even before supper, lots of good things to eat, but then what to do with the kid sitting next to them. Them because she had moved about and closer to Harry. Harry rolled up his mini-napkin whatever they teach I don't want KIDNAPPER OF JOCKEYS DIES IN POORHOUSE in blue around the edges, pretended to place it in his left hand, opened it to show the child that it had but of course disappeared, but she was too young to care or even to pay attention to understand the concept of disappearance.

"What?"

"I'm not talking to you lady?"

"Sorry. I thought you were." She scowled. She wasn't even paying attention. Nobody paid. Outside a light snow was falling. We took about a dozen of the shrouds and her child, fat-faced with legs like minor-league rolling pins, bit her lip and tipped her mother's glass of beer over. "You little...." and Old Man Wellman continued to listen, without missing a beat, nor without kissing one either, to two women who thought they were the latest in French fashion. "Get away from me. Look what you did. Look at the mess you're always causing."

You can always rationalize anything you lose at the track Wambaugh thought, helping himself to his second whatever it was it all tasted like soapsuds. Don't you ever rinse these glasses? If you drop twenty bucks, you can pretend you bought yourself a fancy meal.

Here, play with these! The mother thrust some coasters into the child's hands.

LOOSE LIPS SINK SHIPS. If you drop a few hundred, you can pretend that you went on a vacation to some deserted island. Printed in blue around the edge of the coasters. My buddies were only fifteen years old at the time and by the time the police caught up with us, the women had been wearing their dresses nearly a month turned them around and around in her hands. If you drop a few thousand he was more tired than he thought and not fair because it was only five thirty in the afternoon, you could pretend that your business firm had gone under, or your wife had bought a mink coat or you owed fifty years of back taxes for not declaring your investments in toxic waste. No matter how much you lost, you could always think of some other way the money could have been taken away from you. There were places that you could go to learn what you wanted to learn, but they weren't places anybody ever heard about. You just couldn't write away for a catalog and enroll, but whatever you lost came back in ways undreamed of. For example, the FBI could print coasters with photos of the most wanted on them. One more million-dollar idea. BOOOOOOOM!

Ended up in reform school Wellman said, mopping up the beer LOOSE SHIPS SINK LIPS. But what did the stoplight care? She moved to a stool next to Wambaugh. "My old man couldn't even commit suicide right," she said.

"What?"

"Nothing."

Wambaugh, feeling sorry for the woman, put some money on the counter and bought her another beer. Fill out those tits with a good head. "The kid want another ginger ale?"

"Naah," the woman said, tossing back her red hair, bobby pins in her teeth. Rapunzel, Rapunzel, let down your glorious hair. "She's easy to please. Comes to bars with me to watch television. Besides I can't really leave her at home in the crummy apartment. The social worker got on my case for doing that once. Roaches crawling all over her. We used to have one at home but my old man took it with him when he left. What kind if a guy takes the television set with him when he walks out? Don't men ever think of anything but themselves? Of course, they don't. They never do. Their mothers let them suck at their breasts and all of a sudden they think they're God's gift to women."

Wambaugh's heart sank. Another divorce story. On the television screen over the bar two Chinamen were helping a robot build an atomic bomb in a basement. BOOOOOOOOOOOOOOOOOOM! What a way to go. Rapunzel, Rapunzel, let down your golden nipples. "When the women found out theywere wearing shrouds, they fainted dead away," Wellman said to the television screen. Two women and one man.All manner of obscene acts. What did the child make of it? "I guess children today have brains like television sets," Wambaugh said to the woman. "If they don't like something they just click over to something else."

"I guess." The woman sighed. She picked up her beer. "Me too." The child sipped from her mother's dirty glass. "Couldn't even commit suicide right, the bastard," the mother repeated. "The bastard," the girl echoed. She spoke directly to the golden liquid in the glass. Wellman was talking to the television set. Half the world spent half its time talking to objects without mercy. "Must have been depressed." Booom! What a way to go.

A man with a television set strapped to his back, a modern Quasimodo, convinced a woman to come home with him and to pose for him nude. He pulled off the woman's slacks and she was wearing nothing but a little red silk heart covering her tunnel of love. What a way to go. I'm not that drunk or stupid the woman said looking at the show. Hah! The Evening News was getting stranger all the time. "Climbed to the top of the Masonic Temple. Carried the goddamn TV with him too," the woman said. "When I was a kid," Wellman said to Dan Rather, "I walked into this general store that was selling firecrackers and set a match to an entire display."

Hotter than a firecracker. The man with the television camera placed his hand under the red heart. "How come?" the bartender asked, "that whatever I do never makes news? Tell about selling shrouds as evening dresses. Tell about that."

"Want to play a game?" Wambaugh asked.

"What kind of a game?" the woman asked. "Should I cover up the kid's ears?"

"Just come up with film titles that have the word MURDER in them."

"Sounds like a lot of fun." The woman gave her child her comb to play with. The child dipped it into her ginger ale glass and stirred the bubbles around. Good kid, Wambaugh thought. Doesn't give anyone a lot of trouble. Didn't annoy any of the other customers only him.

"Jumped off the 12th floor of the Masonic Lodge in Cleveland, but on his way down he hit a ventilation duct and landed on somebody's roof. It's hard to respect somebody," the woman said, "if he can't even commit suicide right. Broke the TV set though. Smashed it to hell, so the kid and I have to come in here to get the news."

Why does everything have to happen in Cleveland, Wambaugh thought. Why can't I hold this woman's breasts in my hands? "Smashed it," the kid repeated like a three-foot parrot. Could at least take the jacket off her. Poor kid is probably overheated. Fondle them like that guy with camera strapped to his back? Look, honey," the woman said to Wambaugh, giving him a smile, promising him riches. Boom. "I gotta call the hospital to see if the bastard is all right."

"The one that went off the roof?"

"Yeah. Maybe he still has the warranty on the TV set. Would you mind watching the kid for a few minutes? I'll be right back."

Wambaugh didn't say anything. On the television screen the sky was filled with fireworks and flying nuns. "Momma will be right back," she told her daughter. "This nice man will buy you another ginger ale." The Pope was making a visit to some night class where you couldn't get arrested.

"I don't want another ginger ale." When she pouted a person could see the family resemblance. And all that red hair. Red haired women promised so much. The woman picked up her black pocketbook blessed by the Pope. "I gotta call daddy." Wambaugh stared at his reflection and sighed. Maybe if I am nice to her I'll get lucky. "You should have seen all those skyrockets going through the store. Boy was the owner mad. No wonder I spent so much time in reform school," Old Man Wellman told the drunks at the other end of the bar who held onto every word like men on the flying trapeze.

"The bastard," the girl said, looking at Wambaugh.

"Yes, the bastard," the woman was going out the door, but she returned to get her comb, wiped it on her slacks, and then went out the door again. Wambaugh evaluated the odds of getting his own hands under the red heart. You could have all the skill, all the talent in the world but there really is no substitute for luck.

"The Karate Kid," the bartender said.

"I already have that one."

"The bastard," the kid repeated, and then she didn't say anything anymore, except Mommy Mommy Mommy in a sing-song. "Mommy will be right back," Wambaugh told her.

But Mommy didn't come right back. Wambaugh studied his watch. The woman had been gone for over 45 minutes. "Does your mother always make such long phone calls?" he asked the girl. "I don't know," the girl said.

"What?"

"I have to go to the bathroom."

"Can you go by yourself?"

"Mommy goes with me."

"That may be, but Mommy's not here," Wambaugh said. "When she gets back, she'll take you to the bathroom."

"I can't wait that long."

Wambaugh stared at the clock behind the bar. In red neon the lights spelled out LOOSE SLIPS SINK KIDNAPPERS OF JOCKEYS. Wambaugh got off the barstool and helped the kid down. Her sweatpants were soaked from dribbles of ginger ale.

"Here I'll take you to the men's room." He looked around the bar and all the faces were watching him. What was he doing taking a four-year-old child into a men's room. Pervert.

"I don't want to go to the men's room."

"Well, I can't go to the ladies' room." Not that either of the room were any great shakes. Filth from one end to the other and some wise goy drawing Nazis insignias over the paper towel dispenser. LASSIE EATS CHICKENS. Lots of numbers to call if you wanted a blow job, or if you needed to repair a Masonic ventilation duct.

"I got out of that store so fast that the owner never knew what hit him. About a thousand dollars worth of firecrackers up in smoke."

Wambaugh asked a blonde with a partially opened white blouse if she wouldn't mind taking the little girl to the restroom.

"What?"

"She has to go."

"So take her yourself. Take her to the men's room."

"She won't go to the men's room."

"What's this? A new kind of come on?" The woman dressed in the finest shrouds money could buy had been belligerent because of the drink. Her lipstick was smeared, and her eyes red. One more divorce case in a world filled with divorce cases.

"This your daughter?" another woman asked.

"No." Wambaugh confessed. "I'm just looking out for her."

"By bringing her to this dump?"

"Watch your mouth." Wellman said.

"I gotta go to the bathroom," the little girl said, hopping from one foot to another.

"All right, all right," the blonde with the smeared lipstick said. "But you had better be here when I get back. The least you can do is buy me a drink for doing your dirty work for you."

"It's not my dirty work!" Wambaugh looked out the window. Across the street, there was a payphone but nobody was standing there. With his freight car of a heart loaded with chicken wings, Wambaugh turned back to the bar where Wellman had started in on his Cleveland story again. For gods sakes give it up. "Anyone know where the mother of that little girl lives?" Wambaugh asked in a loud voice?

No response. Like being in a night class with the Pope. What could he expect? Another year of back taxes. "Try Wallach's down the street. Or The Loose Lips Tavern," Wellman suggested. "She was so out of it she probably got confused what bar she left her kid in. " KID

GALAHAD. No, he had done that one. "She goes from bar to bar anyway. You'll find her."

Sure. And I'll find the Holy Grail while I'm at it at the same time. MURDER AT A GALLOP. MURDER WILL OUT. Murder the bitch when I get my hands on her. When she gets back she had better put out for me for what I've done for her. Wambaugh slapped a ten-dollar bill on the bar. "Buy the ladies another round, or fifty of them," he said, and he went out onto the sidewalk. The snow up and down the white layered streets lurked no one resembling a mother or a polar beer or a truant officer. Beer coasters with the racing odds on them.Or news stories. Have to be printed new every day. Lady come on come on snow was falling heavier now. Sober.

There was a tug at Wambaugh's pant leg and then some woman like a needle being dragged across a 33 and 1/3rd long-playing record of Elvis singing:

> I went to the river and I couldn't get across.
> I jumped on an alligator, thought it was a horse.
> I spurned him with my heels, and he began to roar.
> I nearly burned the water up a-getting to the shore.

"Okay you crumb-bum, what do you think you're doing?" the Blonde alligator asked. "You think you can buy my friend and me a drink and stick me with Shirley Temple for the rest of the evening. Take your daughter and whatever she is. And take your crummy ten dollars. I have had it with stinkaroos like you." She tossed the bill into Wambaugh's face and it fell into the snow, where the four-year-old retrieved it.

"I was just standing in the snow," Wambaugh said. "Is there any law against standing in the snow." The woman had gone inside. He could see her through the large plate glass window where it said in gold letters TOPLESS HORSES, NAKED STUDS, HALF-EATEN CHICKEN WINGS. "Let me take you to the bathroom sometime," Wambaugh said when he and the girl went back inside, out of the snow, with only a light spring jacket on her, her mother is out of her mind, clearly nutso, dressing her daughter like that.

Blondie laughed. "I'm not that drunk or stupid. So let you get your hands on my panties."

At the far end of the bar, Quasimodo with a camera strapped to his back was trying to get a nun to undress and pose nude for him. On the other set Fred the Lesbian Salesperson was offering a radio as small as a key chain for only $19.95. If you called in right away, the entire population of Cleveland would be tossed in free of charge. Wambaugh put the girl on a barstool, and turned her head away from the scene of two cops raping a black woman in the back of their patrol car.

"Another ginger-ale."

"No, thank you."

It only goes in one end and out the other. The girl folded her hands and placed them on the wet bar. Her freckled face with its clear blue eyes was perfectly serious. Probably taught to sit that way in Catholic school, Wambaugh thought, counting the seconds. Hell, she's too young to go to school. He himself had gone to Catholic School, but only for the first year. If the nuns could only see him now. What's your name, he asked. "Shirlery," she said. "Shirley what?" "Shirlery Temple," the little parrot said. "It's not Shirlery," he said. "It's Shirley and that's not your real name." "It's my real name," the girl said, making a face like a dead mule. Lower lip drawn out to the edge of doom. BOOOM. "If you're going to sit in a bar you should have some identification," Wambaugh said. When he went to the bathroom, the girl insisted on following him. She was afraid, Wambaugh reasoned, of being left alone. Who could blame her? It was nearly nine o'clock, and still no sign of the redhead with the traffic-light tits. "Identerifashun," the child repeated.

"Why don't you call the cops?" Wellman suggested.

"I can't do that. You know that," Wambaugh said, putting on his coat. He took his white scarf and carefully wound it around the little girl's throat. Murder in the Music Hall. Strangle her and dump the body in the bridle path. The only thing to do.

"Because of the jockey caper."

"Yeah."

Wellman shook his head. Behind him the world was being blown up by a robot, two Chinamen, a pregnant nun, a topless race horse, and a woman with a silk heart for underpants. The five-minute news. "It was only a joke," Wambaugh protested. He looked at the girl's feet. At least the bitch had the sense to clothe her child in snow boots. If it were her child. "If the woman comes back here," Wambaugh says. "Tell her to wait. I'll be back in an hour. Just in case. Or get her name and address." Wambaugh zipped up the girl's blue jacket.

2

Of course there was no sign of her. The Loose Lips Tavern. The Donkey. The Blitz. The 5 in Hand. The trouble with America, Wambaugh thought, was that the bars had such dull names: Joe's, Mike's, The Eagle. In other countries, tavern keepers went to considerable trouble to give their inns a certain air of individuality. They paid good money to sign keepers to paint naked women carried off by swans, or to show Headless Angels in Shrouds. Imagine ordering champagne at the The Inn of Nine Shrouds? Or the Castle of the Blasted Heart.

Every fifteen minutes Wambaugh called Old Wellman for a report, but the bitch the traffic light tits had not returned. No, of course not. Another sucker bet. Just look after her for five minutes. I'll be right back. I'll be back when hell freezes over.

The kid herself didn't look concerned. Maybe she had been through this before. An old hand at being abandoned. At being left in the hands of strangers. Walking out of the Hands of Strangers Bar, "Are you cold?" The girl shook her head.

"Tell me where you live and I'll take you home." A sentence that had been uttered a hundred times if it had been uttered once. But still no reply. The girl in the sweat pants would have been a better accomplice in the Jockey Caper than Maloney and Tischmann. At least she would keep her mouth shut. Hadn't said a word all night long. Wambaugh couldn't even get a name out of her and so he had taken to calling her Shirley. The snow fall settled its lace over the heads of the dead Chinese Robots.

They stood under the movie marquee watching the streets turn white. FORBIDDEN PLANET. Maybe he should take the kid to a movie. She was looking tired. DR. JEKYLL AND MR. HYDE. Exhausted. Her reddish blonde hair was losing its zip. Becoming stringy. Rats tails. As a child he had placed his finger inside a rat's cage and had gotten badly bit. Never had forgotten it. Shirley stood with her hands in her pockets, making circles with her breath. "I can see your breath, kid."

"I can see your breath," the child said. She stood on one leg. Then another. On the corner a twelve-year-old newspaper boy was hawking the local Plain Dealer. Extra. Extra. Read all about it. Murder in the Bridle Path. Also Robert Louis Stevenson's plot for "The Bottle Imp" is found to be plagiarized. The entire story contained in the l823 volume POPULAR TALES AND ROMANCE OF THE NORTHERN NATIONS. That Winchell, Wambaugh thought, he's always on top of everything. Everybody was in some kind of racket. If you can't trust Robert Louis Stevenson, who can you trust? Can't even trust your own mother. Maybe the newspaper boy himself was not what he seemed. Maybe he too had been left on a street-corner by some drunken bozo. Or was he a jockey in disguise, riding his high horse through a world of corruption, bribery, boat races, abandonment, and "You gotta tell me where you live," Wambaugh said. "I'm getting tired. It's gotta be around here somewhere. Right?"

I can see your breath," the girl said, taking her right hand out of her pocket and pointing. His breath was making Rapunzel tits in the air.

"You wanna go home?"

"Okay."

"What do you mean okay?" Wambaugh asked. "Where are we going?"

"I don't know."

FORBIDDEN PLANET. With Robbie the Robot. Even that was based on something else. Some play by Shakespeare. Wambaugh had a collection of Shakespeare's plays at home. He should read it sometime and find out all about the FORBIDDEN PLANET crap. Maybe Shirley would enjoy watching the robot at work. And the killing of the tiger in midair. I wonder how they did that on stage. No wonder everybody called Shakespeare a genius. To disintegrate a live tiger right on the stage.In midair. "You want to go home with me?"

"Okay."

Wambaugh took out his dirty handkerchief and wiped the girl's nose. Her face was ice-cold. Her blue-eyes were ice-cold. Maybe she was like her mother. Had ice-cold water in her veins. "You can't go home with me."

"Why not?"

"Didn't your mother tell you not to go places with people you don't know? You just can't go home with some guy you meet in a bar somewhere. You're too young for stuff like that."

"Like that."

"Right."

"You don't even know my name." Take her into Forbidden Planet, let her fall asleep under the warmth of Cinemascope and flying saucers and then walk out on her, go home and sleep. Let the ushers take care of her., Why not. That's what ushers are for. That's why they carry flashlights. "Harry," she said.

"Right. My name is Harry. What's your name?"

"Shirley."

"That's not your name. What's your last name?"

"Harry."

The kid was impossible. THE KID WAS IMPOSSIBLE. Naah. That wasn't a real one. It didn't count. Harry approached the woman in the ticket-booth.

"What time is the next show?"

"10:15."

Ten-Fifteen. He had been dragging the kid from bar to bar for over four hours. Goddamn bitch. A four hour phone call? I hope she has to pay for it by selling her body to malignant cancer-ridden plague-ridden pus-faced putrid shitheads.

"Forbidden Planet."

"No. Jekyll and Hyde with Spencer Tracy." The woman in the cage was about a hundred years old. No teeth. Revival houses were going down the drain. No hope. No hope anywhere down the line. What's a four year old kid going to make of some guy turning into a werewolf?

"Shit."

"Shit," the girl said.

"Don't talk like that."

"You don't talk like that!" she said, rubbing her gloves over a picture of a robot with a half-naked woman in his arms. Oh what do I care? I'm not her father. I didn't take her television set away from her.

"So who's the heavy date, Waumbaugh?"

Waumbaugh turned to find himself face to face with Police-Sargeant Willoughby Doyle. Doyle in his black slicker and boots had emerged from the movie house.

"What?"

Doyle was laughing at him. He was six foot four and his laughter filled the deserted sidewalk. "I just asked who the heavy date was? You're going after them a little young, aren't you, Wambaugh?"

"Yeah," Wambaugh said.

"Or maybe it's another jockey. You got another jockey on your hands, Wambaugh?" Doyle laughed and tousled the girl's wet hair.

"It's my daughter. That all right with you?"

"Come off it, Wambaugh. You're not married, and you don't have any children. I've read your record. I know more about you than you do."

"I'm babysitting."

"Right. You've got a heart of pure gold. Taking a five-year-old to see Jekyll and Hyde. What are you? Crazy?"

"She's four, not five."

"Well, that makes a big difference doesn't it?"

"What are you bothering me for?" Wambaugh asked. "Why don't you go back inside and watch the movies on the tax-payers time."

"I've seen the movies," Doyle said. He kneeled down in front of the girl and adjusted her jacket. "Not much of a jacket for a night like this."

"What are you? Her mother? You've been out here for two minutes and all you've done is accuse me of kidnapping, not dressing her properly, taking her to movies not suitable for her. If I'm breaking the law, arrest me. Otherwise what business is this of yours?"

"Touchy aren't we? Little girl is this man bothering you? Are you in trouble? You can tell me. I'm a police man."

"And what am I? Jack the Ripper?" Wambaugh exploded.

"Jack the Ripper," Shirley said.

"You both are coming with me," Doyle said, standing up and staring at Wambaugh, the policeman's eyes boring into Wambaugh's soul.

"What?" Wambaugh asked feebly, his right hand reaching for Shirley's tiny hand as she pulled her hand away. Wambaugh's heart sank. It was all he could bring himself to say. "What?"

MY FRIEND GINSBERG

I am going to prove beyond a shadow of a doubt that my friend Ginsberg is not playing with a full deck. A couple of years back, when life offered more opportunities than it does now, Alvin Ginsberg opened a pawn shop on the south side of Fort Lauderdale. Since a lot of old people were using up their life savings just to make ends meet, what with Social Security being inadequate and all, Ginsberg's place filled up right away with jewelry and television sets and even (I swear to God!) sets of false teeth.

My friend Ginsberg would take anything that walked in off the street, and I'm not saying anything about him being Jewish, because right away you would think I was prejudiced. How can I be prejudiced when Ginsberg is my closest friend in all the world. Make that *was*. After the jam he's got me into, Alvin Ginsberg *was* my closest friend in all the world. It only remains to be seen how my friend is going to compensate me for all the grief he's laid on my doorstep—that is if I had a doorstep. Maybe he can bring by, to my trailer, one of those color TV sets he's always promised me.

One day, Ginsberg is closing up shop. He's getting all his cash together to make a deposit at the bank, when in walks this black-haired, brown-eyes Gypsy. I wasn't there you understand. I am telling you what my friend Ginsberg told me in strictest confidence. My friend Ginsberg takes one look at the Gypsy and zing go the strings of his heart. I mean, the poor guy is nearing fifty, he's losing his hair, he makes Sneezy the Dwarf look like

Rudolph Valentino and he thinks God's got nothing better to do than to create earth and to send Ginsberg a big romance, a heart-throb, a *soupçon*, if that is the world, and passion. Passion? Smassion.

"Who are you?" Ginsberg says. "If you got something to pawn, you should show me now, please, because I'm on my way to the bank."

"On the way to the bank?" the Gypsy says. She was wearing a kerchief on her head and had long earrings and lots of bracelets.

All this Ginsberg tells me, so don't go around saying I am prejudiced against Gypsies, too.

"You taking money to the bank?" the woman repeats, nodding her head. She puts down the statue of the Virgin Mary she was carrying in to hock. "Are you Mr. Ginsberg?" she asks.

"I am," says my friend, pulling at his tie.

"Ah, well, Mr. Ginsberg. How lucky for you that I have come to save you."

"Save me?" asks Ginsberg, floating away into the great darkness of her eyes. "I don't need to be saved," he says grimly.

"Ah, but the money! The money! The money!" the Gypsy lady sighs. "May I see the money, please?"

"What are you going to do?" Ginsberg asks me. I say if someone asks to see your money, you play dumb, I say. You run for the police. But not my friend Ginsberg, with the strings of his heart playing the dance of the Sabers. He reaches into his pocket and pulls out three thousand dollars, give or take a few tens and twenties. The Gypsy takes one look at the money and turns pale as death. Pale as death. That's Ginsberg's description. Not mine. To hear Ginsberg tell the story is enough to break your heart.

"What's the matter?" Ginsberg asks the woman.

"That money is cursed," the woman shrieks.

"Cursed?" asked Ginsberg. "What is this *cursed*?"

"Anyone with cursed money is heading for trouble," she says, sitting down on the one folding chair that Ginsberg keeps in his shop, mostly for me, because nobody else stays very long. Just between you and me, Ginsberg's shop is not the cleanest place in the world. Ginsberg thinks about women, but he doesn't think about dust.

"Do you have a handkerchief?" she asks.

"A clean one?"

"Whatever you got," the Gypsy answers. Anyway, these are the words Ginsberg tells me later. Much later.

My friend Ginsberg pulls out his snot rag and hands it to the woman. He's apologetic, but it's the only hankie he's got. I can tell you, whatever romance is possible between a Brooklyn Jew and a Gypsy from Nowhere is destroyed by that handkerchief. But she's got work to do. She takes the handkerchief and tells Ginsberg to put his money on it.

Alvin, the schmuck, half out of love, half out of fear of the Gypsy curse, half out of complete ignorance of human behavior, deposits his hard-earned bills in the handkerchief. The Gypsy folds the handkerchief around the stack of bills, makes a few magic passes, walks three times around the chair, and recites some hocus-pocus-mumbo jumbo, hands the handkerchief with the money back to my friend and tells him that the curse has been removed. Still, to be absolutely safe, Ginsberg should not open the handkerchief for three days.

"Three days?" asks Ginsberg, gulping, stuffing the money in the handkerchief back into his pocket." Three whole days?"

"Three days," the Gypsy says, smiling at him. Ginsberg's heart melts. "I'll be back in three days. Then everything will be in order. You are now safe from harm. You are free from the curse."

"How can I thank you?" asks Ginsberg. "May I buy you supper?" he asks.

"In three days. Then we can celebrate together," the Gypsy says. And then she's gone. She doesn't even take the Virgin Mary with her. My friend Ginsberg takes that as a good sign.

Two days go by, and finally my friend Ginsberg tells me about the Gypsy and the curse and his big date. Right away I'm suspicious. I may not be Einstein, but I'm no ding-dong. Right away I convince him to close up shop, forget about the watches and the false teeth, and together we drive in my Cadillac over to his apartment.

Safely inside 3G (a number I take as an omen) my friend pulls out his bureau drawer, the top one with the underwear in it, takes out the cursed handkerchief. It is tied into a simple knot. He feels the bills wrapped up in it. His hands are shaking so much that he can't untie it, so he gives it to me. He's as pale as a ghost, and so I tell him to sit down.

He sits down, but he stands up again. "It's got to be all there," he keeps repeating. "She had an honest face." "So did my first wife," I tell him, but she did me dirt all over the lot. I open the handkerchief. And there it is. Not the three thousand dollars, just a twenty dollar bill sitting on top of a stack of blank papers cut into dollar bill size. Three thousand dollars in exchange for a twenty. Not bad for less than an hour's work. Ginsberg is out $2,980. And only if the twenty is not a phony, which it most likely is. Some sweetheart, that Gypsy. She had gone and pulled the old switcheroo on him. Ginsberg takes one look at the blank paper, clutches at his heart, and collapses to the floor.

The next thing we are riding in an ambulance. Ginsberg looks like death warmed over, but at least he's breathing. Hardly. Life has pulled the switcheroo on him.

And so there he is, my friend Ginsberg, lying in the hospital for two weeks, and I'm going every day to see him, because he doesn't have any family and I'm all he's got. I'm not getting any younger, and some day I may need a friend myself. Family he doesn't have. But he does have a nurse. The nurse is a real looker. Tall. Blond. Thirty. Maybe thirty-five. I could fall for her myself, but I don't, because if Ginsberg is paying $100 a day, then I say, let him have the luxury of at least falling in love with his nurse, though now I could bite out my tongue for saying so. Zing go the strings of Ginsberg's heart. But this time, it is serious. If I had known how serious, I would have moved to Arizona and gone to live with my sister. Jane is the name of the nurse. Calamity Jane I call her. Maybe he is in love with her because she sticks needles into his bare bottom.

When I drive Ginsberg home from the hospital, he has lost a lot of weight. He says it's from love. I say it's from the hospital food. It's a tossup who is right, except when I'm in love, I eat like a horse. But then me and Ginsberg have about as much in common as a pastrami and a coal salesman.

"Oooooh," Ginsberg says. Day and night, sitting in his little one-room apartment, which isn't even near the breach. "Oooooh." I'm going out of my mind listening to him moan. His lovesick cries take the edge off our gin game.

"What's the matter with you, Ginsberg?" I tell him. "So you lost three thousand dollars. It's only three thousand dollars."

"Only three thousand dollars? Are you out of your mind?"

"At least you learned a lesson. At least you're alive! Some people get killed for three thousand dollars!" Oooooh," says Ginsberg, picking up my three of clubs.

"Remember Manny? Two black guys killed Manny, and what did they get? Fifty dollars, if that. And his wife had five kids."

"Oooooh,"says Ginsberg. Some conversationalist!

"I knock with two."

"I'm in love, Harry," he tells me.

"I would never have known," I say. "How much you caught with?"

"I'm telling you, I'm in love," Ginsberg don't even count his cards. I have to count up my own points and write them down on the pad. 32.

"I'm being sarcastic," I say.

"I'm not," he says.

End of discussion.

Two days later, I'm sitting on the one lousy chair in his pawn shop, holding the statue of the Virgin Mary in my lap. My friend Ginsberg won't sell the thing because as long as he holds on to it, he has hope that the Gypsy will come back with the three G's. You got more hope that a horse with three legs should run the Kentucky Derby and win.

Ginsberg is moaning, walking around like a moonstruck calf. "What are you going to do?" I ask.

"I gotta see that nurse again," he says, staring out into the street, hoping that the blond nurse with the big knockers is going to float on by, singing, "Don't Let the Moon Hit Your Eye." He's got better hope that the Gypsy's going to return and you already know my feelings about that.

"Get sick," I tell him.

"I did," he says. "I thought I was going to throw up, so I went over to the hospital looking for her."

"They're not going to put you in the hospital because you think you're going to throw up," I tell him. "You got no brains, Ginsberg!"

"I asked around for her. Nurse Jane Gilman…." He repeats the name two or three times. It is a prayer. A psalm, a song. It is a mitzvah. Sometimes he sings it, like he should go on stage or something. The Singing Pawnbroker. There won't be a dry seat in the house.

"She take care of you?" I ask, tempted to throw the statue at his head, but I don't, knowing it would be sacrilegious to kill a Jew with the Virgin Mary. Now don't go around saying that I'm prejudiced against the fish-heads either. I'm not prejudiced against nobody, except maybe Ginsberg, and that's only because he's my pal and in love.

"They moved her down to the Emergency Room," Ginsberg says.

"Call her up," I tell him, but it's too sensible for

Ginsberg.

"I can't do that. She don't know me from Adam."

"Of course she knows you from Adam. She nursed you, didn't she? She's seen your naked bottom more than your mother did."

"Just twice. I'm just a name on the chart to her. I've got to show her the real Alvin Ginsberg." He stops his pacing and pauses before one of his glass cases. Maybe there is glass under all the dust.

"Then you got to get into the Emergency Room. Why don't we just drive over and sit around the Emergency Room until she comes out?"

"And make me look like a schmuck?" Ginsberg says. "What am I going to say, just sitting around the Emergency Room? They got a guard and everything." He moves a pistol from the case.

"Alvin, what are you doing?"

"All day long I've been thinking. I think: Ginsberg you're going to shoot yourself in the foot. And then you'll have to go over to the Emergency Room. The beautiful blonde nurse with the big blue eyes is going to see me in such pain, such outright misery, that her heart will melt."

"She'll pity you," I say, not taking my eyes off my friend. Ginsberg with a pistol is like a shark with a hernia. A dangerous combination."

Pity is only a breath away from love. Miss Gilman and I will be together. She will say, "Mr. Ginsberg, how did you wound your foot?"

"And you're going to say that you shot your foot out of love for her?" One more friend like Ginsberg and I can open my very own looney bin.

"Are you out of your mind?" Ginsberg shouts,

waving the pistol dangerously.

"Are you out of *your* mind?" I ask Ginsberg.

"I'm going to tell her that hoodlums tried to break into my store. Four hoodlums. Six hoodlums. And that I drove them out, and one of them shot at me."

"Six hoodlums?" I ask. "What are you? Superman?"

"She'll see me as a hero! How can she not love a hero?"

"Put the gun away," I tell him. I tell it to him from behind the chair. I hold up the Virgin as a shield. If the Virgin Mary isn't going to protect me from a stray bullet, who will?

"No, I'm not," he says, turning the gun around and pushing the handle toward me. "You are."

"I am what?"

"You're going to shoot me in the foot," Ginsberg says.

"Then you can put me into your car and rush me to the Emergency Room. Here. Take the gun."

"I'm not going to take the gun."

"Do you want me to be happy?" he asks. "All my life, I have been miserable. I am close to ecstasy. I can smell her perfume now."

I don't say anything. Nurses don't wear perfume. Their patients could be allergic, like I am suddenly growing allergic to Ginsberg and his ideas of courtship.

"Have I ever asked you for anything? You, my friend? Have I? How can this hurt you? Just point at my foot and pull the trigger, and God will bless you. I will bless you. You will bless you. I guarantee. You will be the best man at my wedding!"

I don't say anything.

"Say something to me, Harry. I'm begging you. Look at me. I'm begging you like we was brothers."

I look at him. "Yeah. Like Cain and Abel." But now my friend Ginsberg is kneeling down on something that resembles a floor. A gun in one hand, a prayer in the other. What am I going to do? The poor man is love starved. He's been swindled out of three grand, he's suffered a heart attack. Perhaps he's right. Maybe the best thing I can do for him is shoot him in his Achilles' heel. "Give me the gun," I say. "I'll deliver you to your beloved on a silver platter."

"Oh, Harry," he says, "I could kiss you."

"Don't bother," I say. "There are some things in life I can live without. "Save your strength for Nurse Knockers."

"Where do you want to shoot me?" he asks.

"Out by the car, so I don't have to carry you," I tell him. "But not now. Later. When there's no one around."

"You're stalling," Ginsberg says. "You think I'll forget!"

"I'm not stalling. Do you want me to get arrested?"

"You're not going to get arrested."

"This is Fort Lauderdale. A gunshot will wake up the neighbors."

"What neighbors?"

"Suppose a policeman comes by?"

"I'll tell him it's not your fault. It's all my idea. Blame me!"

"Thanks."

Ginsberg gets towels to soak up the blood, but when I see how dirty the towels are, I think it's better that he just lets the blood run out. It's then I think I should blow my own brains out.

Ginserg turns around the cardboard sign to read CLOSED. We go out, pulls down the gray window gate, and locks up the store.

"What's the matter?" Ginsberg asks, when I stop, and walk away from my Cadillac. Just like the kind Elvis gives away.

"We're going to use your car. You're not going to bleed all over my Cadillac. You know how much that Cadillac cost me?"

"Am I going to bleed a lot?" He slows down.

"I don't know. How do I know? I've never shot nobody before."

"You're just supposed to wound me," he says. "What are you going to aim for? Tell me what you're going to aim at." He looks frightened.

"I'm going to aim at your heel."

"A heel is dangerous." Good, I think. Maybe he'll come to his senses.

"You want me to shoot you in the toe? You go into the Emergency Room with a bleeding toe and you'll look ridiculous. Nurse Knockers is going to laugh in your face."

We stop in front of his beat-up Buick. "Don't call her Nurse Knockers," he says. "I don't like it."

"You started it," I say.

"Show respect," he says.

I open the door on the rider's side and push him inside.

"Sit down and don't move."

"You get far away," he says. "Stand back. I don't

want you shooting me so close. Get away."

"What am I? Buffalo Bill?" I back off a couple of feet.

"You're just supposed to nick me. Don't hurt me," he whimpers.

"Do you want to do it yourself?" I study the pistol. It's a tiny one. Feels like a cap pistol. I don't know. I don't know guns from canaries.

"Stop punishing me, Harry," my friend Ginsberg wails. "Just do it. Get it over with. Why are you punishing me?"

"Get me to the hospital on time," I sing.

"Very funny."

"Take your shoe off."

"Which one?"

"Either one."

"You're right, Harry. No sense ruining a good shoe." He removes his left shoe and tosses it over the back seat of his car.

"Don't hit me in the foot," he says, changing his mind and standing up. One shoe on and one shoe off makes him look silly. Not romantic at all.

"Why not?" The Florida sun is very hot and I am beginning to sweat.

"Because I want to walk again. A foot wound could be serious. Suppose it injured me for life."

"How about I shoot you in your Johnson and save your nurse a fate worse than Death."

"Are you out of your mind?"

"Me?" Knowing Ginsberg is another Fate worse than Death.

"Wherever you want it," I tell him. "Just tell me." I

open the chamber to the pistol and make certain it's loaded. "I'm taking orders. Point me a spot."

"In the calf, shoot me in the calf," Ginsberg says. He stands by the open door and turns his side toward me. I adjust the pistol, and take aim. My friend puts his right hand over his eyes. He puts his left hand over his left ear to protect himself from the noise. He stands with one shoe on and one shoe off. All this for love I think. What a rotten deal love is. I wait for him to roll up his pant leg.

"The calf is soft," Ginsberg says. I pull the trigger. Ginsberg falls into his car, grasping his leg and moaning. I run forward and help him get adjusted on the front seat. "Put the towels around it," I say. "Keep the towels on it. We'll be at the hospital in no time."

"You hit me in behind the knee," he moans.

"What am I? Buffalo Bill?" I say.

"Aarraghuh," he says.

"Give me the car keys," I tell him.

"Hurry!" he pleads.

I can tell from his eyes that he's in great pain, but there's nowhere I can go without car keys. I crawl onto the front seat from the driver's side and go through his pockets. Pawn tickets. Hankie. Two paper clips.Movie ticket stub.A tiny bar of soap from the Lauderhill Motor Lodge. No car keys.

"In the store," Ginsberg gasps, pulling on my shirt collar. His leg is covered with blood. I take the store key and look up in time to see the black face of a police officer staring through the windshield. He's got a gun pointing at my head.

"Toss your gun out the window," a second voice orders.

I don't think twice. I toss the gun out the window.

"But, Officer, you don't understand."

"Did you hear what my partner said?" the black man asks.

"I'm wounded," Ginsberg cried. "I'm dying."

The black man pushes me against Ginsberg's car, orders me to spread, and frisks me. Not too gentle neither. I see a white man going over to Ginsberg.

"Tell him, Alvin. Tell him it's not my fault," but I guess Ginsberg can't hear me because he's got his own problems and because the black policeman behind me is reading me my rights.

"We're friends," I say.

"Just another lover's quarrel," the white man says. He calls in for an ambulance.

"Emergency Room," Ginsberg pleads. "Emergency Room."

"Don't worry," the white cop tells Ginsberg. "You're going to be all right. We'll get you to the nearest hospital."

Ginsberg sits up and waves his arms. "No, no. Not the nearest hospital. They've got to take me to Broward General. Emergency Room. Emergency Room."

Ginsberg, babbling madly about Broward General, is helped by the white cop. He tells my friend to lie back on the car seat and with a first aid kit, he manages to improvise a tourniquet on Ginsberg's leg. Once Ginsberg is settled, the black cop claps the cuffs on me and pushes me toward the squad car.

"I did it as a favor to my friend," I yell.

"Don't do him any more favors," the black man says, "You've done him enough favors already."

"Tell him it's not my fault," I beg Ginsberg.

"Tell the ambulance drivers to take me to Broward General," Ginsberg shouts after me, and then we hear the sirens.

"What hospital will they take me to?" Ginsberg asks.

"He has insurance at Broward General," I tell them. "He can only afford treatment at the Emergency Room at Broward General." If I don't help Ginsberg, Ginsberg won't help me and I'm the one on the hook.

"Nurse Jane Gilman. I've got to have Nurse Jane Gilman."

"She's the only nurse who understands his particular ailments," I say.

But he cops pay us no mind.

"My friend has a very peculiar anatomy," I shout. "Only Nurse Jane Gilman can help him. Take him to Nurse Jane Gilman!"

"Will you two pipe down?" the white cop says. "Save your song and dance for the ambulance drivers."

"Heart transplant," Ginsberg insists.

"That's right. My friend is the only living Floridian with a heart transplant. That's why he has to go to this special hospital." "Yeah?" Where's his medical tag?" the black cop asks.

The ambulance enters the parking lot with lights flashing, siren blaring, and clusters of onlookers gathering for the entertainment.

"If this man dies," I scream at them, "it will be your fault. Can you live with that on your consciences?"

The white cop takes off his cap and shakes his head. "That's a hot one. You hear that, Elmer? The sonuvabitch shoots him and now it's our fault."

"Ain't that the way?" Elmer says.

"But you don't know the reason!" I say.

"Save it for the judge," the white cop says.

"Emergency Room," Ginsberg begs. I look at my friend and see big fat tears rolling down his face, and I know that he's not crying because of the pain in his leg.

The ambulance drivers examine the tourniquet and agree the cop did a good job. Then out comes the stretcher.

"I'll pay you," Ginsberg says. "Take my money, but take me to Broward General. I'll pay you."

"Heart transplant victims have to be taken to Nurse Jane Gilman," I shout out to the ambulance drivers. "Why would I lie to you?"

"That's right," the white cop says. "Killers are the most trustworthy people on the face of the earth. Their word is gold." Elmer opens the back door to the squad car and pushes me in. He unlocks the handcuffs and then refastens the handcuffs to a steel bar for safe keeping. I'm not comfortable, that's for sure.

I hear Ginsberg shouting. "I'll sue for malpractice."

But my friend Ginsberg, realizing that he's not going to be driven to the arms of his beloved, has passed out. Whether out of anticipation of an ecstasy that is not going to come to pass or from leg pain or from heart-strain or from loss of blood, I have no idea. The mathematics of pain can be a lifetime study. But I couldn't care less. If I weren't handcuffed to the squad's car's restraint bar, I would have strangled him. Strangled him right under the noses of the cops.

So that's how I end up in the Broward County Jail,

and how my friend Ginsberg missed a shot at the nurse with the knockers.

But if you don't think reality is strange, then listen to this. After several weeks of legal maneuvering, and a confession from my friend, I got off with a severe reprimand, 60 days of community service, and a fine.

In addition, one month after my trial, while I was dishing out soup in a church kitchen, Ginsberg finally manages get himself over to Broward General and he finds Nurse Jane Gilman, the true nurse for his heart-ache. Someday soon I bet he's going to remember where I am and call me up to tell me he's going to get married. He's going to ask me to be his best man. Then he's going to name his first child after me. And then I'm going to be a godfather. All because of some Gypsy somewhere. If I ever get hold of her, I'm going to end up back in the slammer for good.

It's written in the tea leaves somewhere.

Ah, Ginsberg. Ah, sweet mystery of life.

SHEATHED BAYONETS

Sheathed bayonets. Abe Fortas had resigned and I was resigned to my Fate, whatever that Fate may be. Eschatology. I allowed Simon and Garfunkel to blow out my ears with "Where Have You Been, Mrs. Robinson?" To some other world? There was music in the air everywhere. Oh, we shall overcome.

VISION OF HELL (WESTERN IRELAND)

I have seen hell myself. I had a sight of it one time in a vision. It had a very high wall around it all of metal, and an archway in the wall, and a straight walk into it, just like what would be leading into a gentleman's orchard, but the edges were not trimmed with box but with red hot metal. And inside the wall there were cross walks, and I'm not sure what there was to the right, but to the left there were five great furnaces and they were full of souls kept there with great chains. So I turned and went away; and in turning I looked again at the wall and I could see no end to it.

An Old Army Man, whose vision is recorded in *Visions and Beliefs in the West of Ireland* collected and arranged by Lady Gregory. New York and London: G.P. Putnam's Sons, 1920, p. 107.

The passage above raises the question: How many worlds do we live in at the same time? None of my friends had been drafted; none had been shipped to Vietnam.

All that I could think about was that it was possible for a young person to stand in the middle of History and have no idea at all what was going on. How small and small minded History could appear. Was there more History or more Future? Who cd. ever know? Whoever said, "Size did not matter" was not referring to all the History piling up since the beginning of time, since the discovery of fire. Or maybe it was the loss of true fire. "Light My Fire" played in my head morning, noon, and night. I was ready to be lit up like a firecracker. Unfortunately, I didn't have enough money to fly off to India to study with the Maharishi Mahesh Yogi. My only Yogi was Berra.

Aoxomoxoa. All the words in the big dictionaries limnology I had lugged home. What good would a spoonful of diamonds do anyone? What need did my mother have for big words? Why don't we go out and chuck berry? Or my sisters.Or the Norse giant Mimir who guards the well at the root of Yggdrasill? Any person who drank of those waters would know the past and the future. It's always the Present that escapes us, eh? Lenny Bruce had died of an overdose of cops. No big words in Wild Thing. No liripipe.

At the time of some of these thoughts—not all (a few occurred to me much later)—were coursing through my mind while my mother and I were standing in the kitchen of our tiny house on Mayo Street in Hollywood, Florida. Heavy winds and even heavier rain (weighed upon whose bathroom scales? Our bathroom scale was always broken) had knocked out the power, and rain (as had been written so many times before in oh so may heavier books) was lashing at our jalousies.

Lashing at our jealousies?

74

Jazz in the penal colony. Yah. Yah. Yah. My mother had lit red candles shoved into the necks of wrecked Chianti bottles, so many dead pirates, with a ho hoho on a dead man's chest so that we could put book covers on a set of three encyclopedic dictionaries I had carted home from New Hampshire.

*   *   *

"And another time I saw purgatory. It seemed to be in a level place and no walls around it, but it was all one bright blaze, and the souls standing in it. And they suffer near as much as in hell, only there are no devils with them there, and they have the hope of heaven."

2

Bring on TuliKupferberg and the Fugs!

What was I doing in New Hampshire? Not to drink at the well at the root of Yggdrasil. I had gone there by bus to fetch my sister who had run away from her husband and now we were both home. My other sister Jean was also home for the night because her 24 yr. old husband Kitch had gone off with two warped and pock marked fishing buddies, and now because of the approaching hurricane named Maharishi Mahesh Yogi he was in for a rough time. Not that I cared. I didn't like him. If you remove the human heart from the body, you might, under optimum conditions, keep the heart alive for nearly four hours. I didn't know nor care if he had a heart. To know him was not to love him. Not by spoonful or by spoonfuls.

3

Illustrative anecdote. My sister, her husband Kitch, and my parents and I had gone to the dog tracks to make our fortune. My father and I were in on the pick four for the final race, but Kitch and Jean had their $2.00 on another dog, and so Kitch was rooting against us, even though my father and I stood to win several thousand dollars. My father drove home in silence, seething, seething. Seething! Smoke from his ears. We had lost, of course. We weren't a family known for winning. Not at money anyway. "How could he root against us?' my father asked. Fuming.

4

The utility room of our infinitesimal house was stacked to the rafters with dog books. If there was a system out there that would allow a single human being to beat the dogs, my father was going to find it. The mathematics was staggering. His was the music of another generation. The Troggs meant nothing to him. No big words in Wild Thing. He hated my long hair and constantly yelled at me to get it cut. Oh, we shall overcome. Someday. Why not now? We needed Grace. How slick was Grace?

My sisters, worrying about the approaching storm, were in their bedroom, listening to a portable radio. There was music in the air everywhere. Oh, we shall overcome. I was four years older than one sister and six years older than the other. The older sister Fran was married but had moved out of her husband's house because he had become abusive.

Jazz in the penal colony. Yah. Yah. Yah.

5

I don't know why my sisters married abusive husbands. Maybe it had to do with my father's Greek personality and his own explosive temper. His own father had once threatened him with a meat cleaver. Clever cleaver. Who needed the words? I waited to live in the Great Society. Sometime later in the 60s (if I could have seen the future, what changes would I have made in my own life?) I met Charlie Mingus. He had bought a new 35mm camera and was having trouble loading the film. I had taken up photography, but now many years later everything is slightly out of focus. I loaded the film for him so he could preserve his past for someone's future, and that was my contribution to the history of jazz. There was this history and that History. Life was this and that. Mostly that. The most a beetle could live would be about three years. What was the life span of a jazz musician? Or an eighteen year old in Vietnam? Would I just be a mere linkboy in the Great Procession?

Earlier in the evening my mother had received a phone call, and Fran's husband had said that he was going to come over to our house to take his wife home. He had a vicious temper. My father was sleeping in the master bedroom, dreaming of God knows what. He had told me a story about being kidnapped by gypsies and taken away to live in a cave, but I didn't know how to make heads nor tails of it. Fathers tell stories that don't make sense to their children until long after the fathers are dead.

I think my father, then in his late fifties, was sleeping in order to conserve his strength for the confrontation that lay ahead. It was one of the reasons sleep was invented. An entire generation had slept through the fifties in order to gather enough strength to face the flaming sixties. Who knows what he was dreaming? I can only tell you what my old man said. He was afraid of dying. And who could blame him? Who besides Robert (I don't know if he had a heart) McNamara could blame any of us? My mother suggested to Fran's husband Dixon that it would better if he didn't come. Fran didn't want to go home with him. Even I, standing three feet away, cutting up paper bags, could hear the fuming at the other end. The seething. The slamming of the telephone receiver. Receiving what?

Oh God, my mother said, putting her hand to her mouth. Her small, underweight frame trembled in the candlelight. She knew something bad was going to happen. So much bad had already happened. Maybe the hurricane would keep everyone at home I suggested. I was lying. She knew I was lying.

6

David Dellinger, chairman of the National Mobilization Committee to the End the War in Vietnam, had suggested that I be in Washington in time for the levitation of the Pentagon. It was just the kind of craziness to engage completely what little imagination I had left. A permit had been issued for such an activity but some wag at the Pentagon had put it in writing that we would be allowed to levitate the Pentagon to a height of only 10 feet. Hell, if 800 or so of us could ring the Pentagon, and, using our brain waves alone, could lift the Pentagon off the ground for only one tenth of an inch, the war in Vietnam would end in a minute. Entire courses of civilization, Western and Eastern, would be forever changed. Give Peace a Chance.

The hero of Being There was named Chance. The world was full of wags and another wag tailing the dog, created a more appealing slogan—Give Chance some Peace.

7

I thought we could raise the Pentagon another way. We would round up millions of cockroaches and slide them under the cracks in the foundation. Lots of cracks in the foundation and another world order carried away on the back of insects.

My mother and I were cutting up paper bags and scotch taping the brown bags to the books, creating pleasing covers. In spite of the storm and the terrible phone call, my mother and I were moderately merry. Maybe it was the cooking sherry she had dipped into. Or the luke-warm beer. If the refrigerator did not come back on, we would have to toss out a lot of food. My parents, having survived the Great Depression, always kept on hand more food than we could possibly eat. But wasn't that what being an American meant—having more of everything than we needed.

Everything except money, of course. It was the grueling lack of money that had given my old man his ulcer, forcing him to spend hours every night vomiting up the food he had consumed or shouldn't have consumed, night after night with the house absorbing his moans and pitches.

We could have used a big win at the dog track.

But his is about my mother and my sisters and me, and not about my father. I can remember only a few other moments in our lives when my mother and I felt so close to the essence of each other's beings. Don't ask me what I mean precisely by that remark, because I don't think I can tell you. I took out slices of bread, placed them on forks, and toasted the bread over candles. Cassius Clay became Muhhamed Ali. Lew Alcinder became Kareem Abdul Jabbar. All I wanted to was to become myself, and I only had the vaguest idea of what that could be. I loved the smoky taste of bread over candles, the ash, bizarre black and whiteness of it all.

8

Hey, LBJ
How many kids
Did you kill today?

9

I had sat through Bonnie and Clyde and had come away from that movie shot through the heart. The Generals had been lying to us about body counts and losses. The body bags piled up. Lies all the way to the

Kingdom of Heaven. Much later I would learn that the excuse to start the war was another great lie.

From Wikipedia:

*It was originally claimed by the National Security Agency that a **Second Gulf of Tonkin incident** occurred on August 4, 1964, as another sea battle, but instead evidence was found of "Tonkin ghosts"[4] (false radar images) and not actual North Vietnamese torpedo boats. In the 2003 documentary The Fog of War, the former United States Secretary of Defense Robert S. McNamara admitted that the August 2 USS Maddox attack happened with no Defense Department response, but the August 4 Gulf of Tonkin attack never happened.*

The outcome of these two incidents was the passage by Congress of the Gulf of Tonkin Resolution, which granted President Lyndon B. Johnson the authority to assist any Southeast Asian country whose government was considered to be jeopardized by "communist aggression". The resolution served as Johnson's legal justification for deploying US conventional forces and the commencement of open warfare against North Vietnam.

10

This is my generation, baby, Peter Townsend of the Who had sung. So much sudden violence, no matter which way I turned. On the day I received my draft deferment in the mail, I had been walking back to the small house on Mayo Street, when I saw green paper fluttering across an open field. When I retrieved the paper, it turned out to be a ten dollar bill. How much more lucky could I get? Free money and a draft deferment, all on the very same day. Perhaps the gods were smiling upon me after all. However, I could never do what Dellinger had done in 1940, when, with eight divinity students, he had refused to register for the draft. Like Robert Lowell, Dellinger ended up in prison. Dellinger, however, had been sent to the Federal Corrections Institute in Danbury, Conn.

I was in another kind of prison. The prison of fear. I was imprisoned by small, tiny cells of my own making. Brain cells.

I had been attending graduate school in New York City and had already lost one wife because she had fallen in love with somebody else. A clarinet player. What a family. I thought. My parents, though thick and thin, toughed out long years together, while my sisters and I were piling up our own body counts.

What is the half-life of a marriage?

What is the half-life of a nation which sends its young people out to die for lies?

11

When Fran and I had returned by bus from New Hampshire, laughing at each other's jokes from one state into another, from New Hampshire to the state of confusion and confession and affection, my father insisted that we all drive over to our youngest sister's house and surprise her. And this we did. Jean and her husband Kitch were living in a small apartment in a row of single level white stucco apartments only a few blocks from my parents' tiny house on Mayo Street. Everything in the world was beginning to seem smaller to me, smaller than it should be. The apartment complex looked a lot like a short-stay motel.

I knocked on the door and then we waited. We waited for what seemed like a long time. I knocked again. Jean finally opened the door, took one look at me and Fran and my parents and burst into tears. Tears flowed out in great gobs, tears so thick that Jesus himself could walk across him. We were forming a new lake of tears, and a choppy lake it was. Behind her a radio played *sha da dada*. Kitch, we eventually learned, had been in a foul mood all afternoon and they had been fighting. So much for ever surprising my sisters again, I thought.

But what were the 60s but one surprise after another? Bizarre, black and whiteness of it all. Yip. Yip. Yip.

12

I had marched against the war. With what I know now I can say the lying war. And we did not win it because there was nothing to be won.

Hell No we won't go. Indeed I had done a bit more than March. I had purchased a 16mm Bolex from a pawnshop and I had started filming in black and white the marches. I thought I would put together a documentary. That would be my minuscule contribution to the history of film, the history of History. What a laugh! I never got around to editing the material, its accumulations of sit ins, police actions, obscene gestures, chants, folk songs, manifestoes, resistances.

Those films in brown metal containers are now rotting in a cardboard box under my desk at the newspaper office on Broad Street in Philadelphia. From History to journalism in a few brief years. Is that a series of baby steps? Or is it a giant leap for mankind?

The small lab where I had my film developed was run by a tiny black-haired lady whose husband had recently died. She was Filipino and sympathetic to independent film makers, so much so that she frequently let us have our film before we could pay for it. One of the film makers whom I had met casually had skipped town with a debt of over $6,000. The woman kept asking me if I knew where she could reach him. I had no idea. I had very few ideas about how to reach anybody. Bring on McNamara and the Thugs. The 60s were going to turn belly up for her company too. My heart was breaking for such people, but there was nothing I could do to help. I had loaned one printer $300, and I had never gotten that money back either. It was money I could ill afford to lose. That was my contribution to the Printing Business. I was spending $55 a month rent on a five floor walkup and living like The Hunchback of Notre Dame. My apartment contained nearly every example of the 3,500 living cockroach species. I had even discovered an albino cockroach. Would that discovery be my claim to fame?

I badly needed money, but I couldn't borrow any from my parents nor my sisters. They had none to spare. A friend of mine had started to edit a film called *No Vietnamese Ever Called Me Nigger*. I wondered if I would make the march on time, and I wondered what would happen if it rained on our parade. Would it be more difficult to levitate the Pentagon under such conditions? Or would it be easier? How would that largest of large buildings float in such a heavy atmosphere, although nothing could have been more heavy than the atmosphere my country had created for itself.

I had marched and had refused to vote. That was my contribution to Anarchy. As far as I was concerned the country was run by criminals, potential criminals, and the inner sanctum of Ivy League cronies who could commit all manner of crimes and get away with them. I saw *The Graduate* two or three times and even read the short novel upon which it was based. The author? Well, his name is mostly forgotten too.

Somewhere on another coast, the grape pickers were on strike, so my friends and I decided to support them by not eating grapes. Big fucking deal. Nixon, when he took office, would later kick the strikers in the teeth by increasing the Defense Department's purchase of grapes from 500,000 pounds in 1968 to 2,000,000 pounds in 1969. The grapes were sent to our troops overseas. I guess Tricky Dick figured that when the soldiers got tired of fighting a war few Americans believed in (decades later some Pentagon high mucka mucks would apologize, admitting the war had been unjust, but what words, little or big, could bring back the dead and erase our grief?) they could celebrate by jumping into a huge tub of grapes, stomping out Saigon Wine, a vintage to be served at room temperature at all White House functions.

I had read *Nigger* and *Conscience of a Conservative*, but didn't finish the second book because any book with the word *conscience* in its title was far beyond my limited abilities to understand. I didn't want a conscience any more. What good was it? As for *nigger*, it was a word I had heard a lot of. The town of Hollywood had been completely segregated. When I went to the beach, there were no black people on the beach. There were no black students in the local high school. Ralph Ellison had been right. It wasn't black and white. It was white and invisible. And now America had found a perfect use for its population of young black males. Ship them off to Vietnam to fight a white man's war of oppression. And then when black soldiers returned home (and the lucky ones returned) they were refused coffee at small town lunch counters. The war was being fought on several fronts at the same time. No Vietnamese Ever Called Me Nigger.

How could I, from my most limited perspective, look into the needs of time from the bottom of a well of current events, and cold currents they were too? And predict that 30 years later I would share my tiny office on North Broad Street with a Vietnam vet, a man who had been a Lieutenant ad had survived the horrors, going on to earn a Ph.D. in Philosophy? The war would always be a gap between us, for he had gone and I had not. He knew so many more important things that I could never know.

13

It was about eleven thirty when Dixon finally arrived. We could hear the car pulling onto the gravel in front of our tiny lawn. And it was raining very heavy. Well water spilled upside down. My old man was still sleeping.

"I had better wake your father," my mother said.

I knew that my father kept a revolver in the house. Maybe 9mm. I didn't know anything about guns. I knew less about houses. As a young child growing up into a life I would no longer recognize going in and out of doors, I had seen the revolver in the top right hand drawer of my father's bedroom bureau. The gun was carefully stored in a small white pouch tied by a white string. There were even bullets. All I had to was to put the bullets into the chamber and I too could put lives in danger. My father would have caught hell if my mother knew that I, as a child, had found the revolver and had found it fascinating. Couldn't I pick up the paper without reading about some child killing himself or a friend? Or a sister.

Maybe Dixon had come armed too. I wouldn't have put it past him. That was what my mother was afraid of. And my sisters.

My sisters, carrying flashlights, they had padded out of the back bedroom and entered the kitchen. They wore blue jeans and loose white shirts borrowed from my father's closets. Jean was the youngest, blonde like her mother, and a bit chubby. I was much closer to Fran, not only in age, but in temperament. We could make each other laugh so easily. But there was no laughter now.

My mother sank down into a kitchen chair and grasped for her rosary beads. "Go wake your father," she told Fran.

"No," I said. "I'll go out there. Let daddy sleep."

"No, no, Louie," my mother said. "You can't go out there. Someone's going to get hurt.

"No one's going to get hurt," I said. "I'm just going to talk to him."

"Call the police," Jean suggested. She was the baby of the family, the one who always panicked first.

"Maybe I should go out there," Fran suggested. "After all he came here to see me." She twisted her long brown hair in her hands.

'You don't have your shoes on," I said, "and I want to head him off before he gets to the door. Besides, he didn't come here to see you. He's come here to get you. There's a big difference." I grabbed a purple, or maybe it was black, umbrella out of the wastepaper basket that served as our umbrella stand, and opened the front door, fully expecting Dixon to be there.

But he wasn't.

It was raining very heavily and he was still seated in his Buick, with the headlights on. It was eerie. His headlights provided almost all the light for the street. The streetlamps were out, and there some flickers of candlelight and flashlights in the neighboring houses. I had lost track of time. But it felt like midnight. Or 2 A.M. in the soul.

Perhaps I had been right after all. Perhaps it was the heavy rain that was giving him second thoughts. The ground was unable to absorb the water spilling out of heaven. Our front lawn with its stunted palm tree had been turned into Lake Victoria. Or Lake Despair. I hadn't taken five steps when the wind had rendered my puny umbrella useless. Actually, it wasn't my umbrella. It probably belonged to one of my sisters. But now it belonged to nobody. It was useless. Laughable. An emblem of my tattered self. I didn't even bother to try to pull it shut, but merely tossed it into the carport and ran toward the Buick.

I knew right away that I would have to go to the car, because I wanted to keep him far away from the house as possible. It was the only strategy I could think of. But if he wanted to force his way into the house, I wasn't quite sure I could stop him. Actually, I knew I couldn't stop him.

But if my father was now awake and was rummaging through his bureau for the revolver—well, that would be even worse. With my sneakers soaked through and water inside my socks, I ran around Dixon's car to the passenger's side and quickly tapped on the windows. He unlocked the door and pushed the door open. I slid inside and slammed the door shut.

"What happened to your umbrella?"

"The wind nearly snapped it off at the handle," I told him, wiping my sleeve against my face. I knew I was going to come down with a bad cold and now would probably miss the march against the Pentagon.

"You look like shit," he said.

"Thanks. I needed that." I found my dirty handkerchief and rubbed it over my hair, trying to get as dry as I could. Maybe if I could keep his attention focused upon me and my failings, he might forget what he came for. Some chance of that!

Dixon was a tall man, six foot two or three, tanned, with arms like small barrels. He was wearing a long wool coat, unbuttoned, over a white T shirt and blue jeans. His left hand still clutched the steering wheel. His right held a can of Budweiser. "Help yourself," he said. There was a six pack between us. He was in his mid-thirties and managed the local Food Fair store so that was about as much as I knew about him. I had only seen him a few times in my life and I met his father once. His father had gotten drunk and kept asking me about my wife, "She's no B girl. I can tell that. Right?"

"Fran inside?"

Ah, the second crises. Tell the truth or lie? Well, no sense in living. He knew Fran was inside. Where else would she be? No, she disappeared. Ran away to Alabama with a clarinet player. A member of the Rotary Club. How do I know? Her taste in men left a lot to be desired.

"She's sleeping," I said.

He didn't respond. Just stared ahead, drinking his beer.

"Must have been tough driving all the way over here." I attempted to hold up my end of the conversation by changing the subject. The less we talked about Fran the better. I didn't want him thinking about Fran. I just wanted him to go home.

"Not so bad," he said.

"Some of the streets must be flooded by now."

No response. I helped myself to a can of beer. He didn't stop me. If we were drinking buddies, maybe he wouldn't hurt me so much. I couldn't decide if he were carrying a gun or not. He looked out of place in his long winter coat. Nobody had a winter coat in Florida. But maybe he chose to wear it because it had deep pockets. I opened the beer and promptly spilled some over myself. Wet upon wet. Was he carrying any weapons?

It was a legend in my family. When my father first took home his future wife, my mother, to meet his mother for the first time, it was the night of a hurricane. His mother invited my mother to spend the night, but my mother, having been brought up properly, could not bring herself to spend the night under their roof. My father had to drive her back home in high wind and rain. I wasn't going to share that with him. He didn't deserve it.

I bit the bullet. "What do you want to do?"

"I want Fran to come back home with me…" He kept staring into the huge rain that lashed the windshield, looking where I was looking, down a wind drenched street where no one was.

Elsewhere there was all kinds of trouble. Later my friends would tell me about the events at the Pentagon. The sinking temperatures. The tear gas. The soldiers in their gas masks carrying sheathed bayonets, and then, as the protests started singing "Down by the Riverside," the soldiers removed the bayonets from their rifles and transferred them to the belts around their waists.

A bayonet. Or a long knife. That's what I should have brought outside. I was sitting close enough to Fran's husband (if I had to say brother-in-law, I would gag) that I could have slipped a shiv between his ribs and saved my sister from a fate worse than death.

"What?" I pretended not to hear. If he had to repeat everything he had said perhaps he would realize just how foolish he was acting.

Make love, not war. How many times had I chanted that? Or "Peace, peace, peace." The protesters built a bonfire for warmth, but still the Pentagon remained rooted to the ground. A few of the younger and more cynical marchers carried banners that read: "Where is Oswald when we need him?" Others carried blue and red flags with a yellow flag in the middle-symbols used by the Vietcong. I never thought that was a good idea.

"*Hell no, we won't go.*"

David Dillinger stood in front of the crowd and announced: "This is a beginning of a new stage in the American peace movement in which the cutting edge becomes active resistance."

I want Fran to come home with me," he repeated.

I sucked air. "I don't think she's going to," I told him, not raising my voice, trying not to move a muscle. Even the beer didn't taste good. "At least not tonight. Maybe if you let things settle for a while. Let her calm down and get her bearings, then she'll probably come back to you."

"You think so?"

"I think so." I was lying through my teeth. "I don't know what goes through women's minds. Do you?"

"I love her so much."

"I'm sure she knows that." I was speaking as gently as I could. I started to shiver. "I loved my wife too."

"I gotta talk to her," he said.

When he opened the car door, I nearly jumped out of my skin. He tossed the beer can into our front lawn and then pulled the door shut. It was, I guess his way of making a political statement.

"I'm sure she wants to talk to you, but not tonight, I told him. I tried not to touch my nose. I had been told that was a sure sign someone was not telling the truth. The generals did it all the time.

"Why not tonight?"

"You know my father's got that terrible ulcer," I told him. I pulled out another can of beer and handed it him. If he got killed on the way home I would be an accessory to a crime. Me and Lyndon Johnson linked by crime. "He's very sick tonight. If you go in there tonight and there's a scene, he'll probably have a heart attack and die. If that happens Fran will never forgive you."

He pulled the tab back on his beer can.

Then Dr. Benjamin Spock got up to speak: "We are convinced that this war which Lyndon Johnson is waging is disastrous to our country in every way and that we, the protesters, are the ones who may help to save our country if we can persuade enough of our fellow citizens to think and vote as we do."

"Tell her to come out."

"I don't want to wake her up."

We pondered our strategies. "Why don't you get your hair cut?" Dixon said. "You look like a fairy."

"Thanks," I said. We were starting to repeat ourselves. "I needed that."

"All you fairies are too scared to go to war yourself. At least I fought in a war. I know what it's like."

"Look," I said. "If you stay here much longer, you're not going to be able to get home. The streets are becoming rivers."

"I'll sleep in the car."

"If that's what you want to do."

"It won't be the first time I done it."

We were like two animals hitting our heads against a stone wall. Trying to break through a line of soldiers, I had been hit in the chest with a rifle butt. I knew what that felt like.

"I laid a lot of women in this car," he said. I believed him. I had no reason not to.

"A lot of women," he repeated.

"Why don't you go home and I'll tell Fran to call you."

"She won't call me. She hasn't called me all week." He sounded like some sort of wounded animal.

"Let me talk to her. I can talk her into calling. She listens to me. I'm her brother."

"She thinks you're a fairy too."

I nodded. It wasn't true. "It would be better for us all if we got it straightened out. I know my parents aren't happy about it. Who wants to have their daughter come back home to live with them? My parents are getting old. They don't need any extra problems." I placed my half-empty beer inside his glove compartment and shoved it shut. I was not going to lecture him about littering. "They got enough of their own."

He crushed the empty beer can in his hand. I waited to see where he was going to throw it. At my head?

"How's your father doing?" I asked. "Last time I saw him he looked good. He's a tough sonuvabitch."

"Those are the ones that live a long time."

He didn't reply. I pushed the door open with my shoulder. "Go home. She'll call you." I jumped out. I made a dash to the house, all the time glancing over my shoulder to see if he was going to follow me. The door had been locked behind me, so I had to ring the doorbell to get in.

My father was up, dressed in his black pants and a white undershirt, and was seated in the kitchen with my mother and sisters.

"We were getting worried about you, Louie." My mother with her glass of beer sat at one end of the black Formica table. My father sat at the other. My sisters stood at the sink, smoking. The candlelight threw all kinds of crazy shadows upon the white walls. Crazy shadows is what we would all eventually become. So much for protecting my sisters.

"What's he going to do?" Fran asked. Even in the faint light I could tell she had been crying. I bet my father had been lecturing her.

"If he tries to break his way into this house, I'll kill the bastard," my father said. I glanced at the table to see if he had brought out his revolver, but there was no gun there.

"Don't talk like that," my mother said. Too sharply I thought.

"I'll talk any goddamn way well I please," my father shot back.

I opened the refrigerator door. It made me feel strange not to find any light inside. All that meat rotting in darkness.

"What were you two talking about all that time?" Jean asked. "You were out there a long time."

"We decided that since Fran didn't want him any longer, I did. We decided to get married." I found a carton of milk, sniffed it. It was still fresh. Warm but fresh. I regretted my joke.

"What's he going to do?" my mother asked.

"I don't know. I think he's going to sleep in the car."

"No, he's not," my father said. "I'll go out there and put a bullet through his head."

My mother took her beer and went to sit in the living room. There were two candles burning in there.

Fran followed her and looked out the window. "I don't see anything," Fran said. "I think he's gone."

"I hope so. For his sake," my father said.

Jean poured some water into an ashtray and rubbed her cigarette out. "Maybe he's parked someplace else and he's sneaking around the back."

"Let's not get paranoid," I said. I was having difficulty finding a clean glass, and then I remembered why I had difficulty coming home. "Fran, I told him if he went home you would call him."

"Your sister's not going to call him," my mother said, lighting another cigarette. The place was turning into a smoke factory.

"I wouldn't if I were her," Jean said.

My father kept rubbing his stomach. The look upon his face suggested he was in deep pain.

"Did anybody from the National Mobilization Committee call?" I asked.

No response.

"Are the phones still working?" I picked up the receiver from the white wall phone and listened for a dial tone.

"I'm glad he didn't hurt you," my mother said.

"No. We just had a good talk," I said. There was a dial tone. At least something worked.

News on the portable radio said that David Dellinger and about 250 others, including Norman Mailer and the Reverend John Boyles, and assistant Episcopal chaplain at Yale, had been arrested. Tear gas had been used against some of the protesters. In spite of it all, the Pentagon did not budge. All that effort for what?

14

And I heard a call to me from Hell. "Help me to come out of this!" And I looked. It was a man I used to know in the army, an Irishman and from this county, and I believe him to be a descendant of King O'Connor of Atrhenry. So I stretched out my hand first, but then I called out, "I'd be burned in the flames before I could get within three yards of you."

So then he said, "Well, help me with your prayers," and so I do.

THE MUSIC CABINET

O.K. I am not that bright. So what? But I know this: the day that Kid McCoy committed suicide was the same day I bought a music cabinet for my wife.

My first wife that is.

That marriage, believe you me, has been over a long time now. Of course, that makes me luckier than some. There are marriages that folded ages ago and the participants don't even know it.

Still I think fondly about that dark mahogany music cabinet and wonder if Tobey still has it. Or has it been sent to the warehouse where Rosebud and other sacred objects of Americana await burning or have been burnt. In spite of the fact that I might well be one of God's more insignificant antiparticles, it does happen every so often amid all the black holes of our universe, in a great spill of light years, a person manages to find the perfect gift for some person you love, and the very perfection of the gift makes your day. Sometimes it even makes your whole year.

The year was 1940 and Tobey and I were living in Detroit. We were both in our mid-20's. She was studying piano at the Conservatory and I was working as the public relations director for the Copley chain of hotels. My wife was enthused about her studies, but I wasn't enthused about the direction my life had taken. Thus, it came to pass as they say in Biblical phraseology, Tobey and I were not getting along. Bitter understatement there, brother, with wit so dry camels would drop dead in it. Our lives didn't overlap enough, and when they did overlap we often had other things upon our minds than each other. Yea, verily. So, after weeks of browsing in second-hand furniture shops, second hand watch stores with their second hand second hands, browsing through second hand sex novels, I stumbled in my stumble-bum manner upon a beat-up mahogany music cabinet, with two dozen slender shelves, shelves perfect for the storage of sheet music.

I bought it.

The cabinet was only twelve dollars used, plus another five dollars to have it delivered to our five floor walk up. I helped the old man who drove the delivery van to carry the cabinet up the stairs. It weighed a ton and the stairs were numerous and narrow, but it was a cool April day and so the task was not impossible. I put it right in the middle of our living room and tipped the old man fifty cents. If you think fifty cents is not much of tip, you have to remember that fifty cents went a lot further in those days. I too went further in those days.

Next I located some huge sheets of drawing paper and, with a black crayon, wrote: FOR TOBEY, HAPPY BITHDAY! LOVE SAM. I wanted my wife to some home, walk into the living-room and to be completely bowled over. It wasn't her birthday, but everybody needs a surprise every once in awhile. That's why God creates tragedies.

I sat on the purple couch and contemplated the cabinet. We needed a new couch more than we needed a place to store music, but people cannot be expected to be practical all the time, especially when the whole world seemed to be getting ready to blow up in our faces. The cabinet had history; it held great promise. I guess one could say the same thing about the world.

Tobey was out giving a piano lesson to someone; I didn't know what time she would be getting home, but I didn't want to be around when she tiptoed in, I would return after my generosity had taken its effect. Not unlike Jack Horner, I thought what a good guy I was, and I was expecting more than a plum for a reward.

The phone rang and that gave me the excuse to get out. It was Roger MacReady, my boss. He was at the Midtown Hotel and he was in a panic because Kid McCoy, the world famous boxer, had committed suicide. He wanted me to come down right away to help fend off the reporters. Hotels never like it when people commit suicide in their rooms.

I didn't know much about Kid McCoy and I could have cared less. I am a baseball fan, not a boxing one, and the Tigers were fielding a pretty good team that year. Later I found out that Kid McCoy had quite a colorful career, both in and out of the ring. He was a flamboyant boxer throwing what some sports writer had cleverly labeled a "corkscrew punch." Don't ask me what it is. I have no idea. I never saw him fight. I just saw him dead. There's a difference. In a nanosecond a person's consciousness is dissipated into nothingness or into some nonhuman particles or something I would never understand or even recognize. Science, philosophy, and *Gone With the Wind* will be, well, gone with the wind.

Somewhere in my collection of baseball cards, parking tickets, and court summons, I have a copy of his suicide note. I don't know why I keep it. Tobey would say I'm too lazy to throw it out. I should throw out the memory of the music cabinet, but I'm too cowardly to allow that memory disappear too. Where would I be without my memories? What would I be without my memories? Just another piece of wax fruit, and nobody would mistake me for the real thing. The Real McCoy, as it were. As opposed to Kid McCoy. I once knew the origin of the phrase "the real McCoy" but I can no longer remember what it was. Memory, what a sleight-of-hand artist the mind truly is.

Whenever I hear people saying that they have no regrets, I know that they're lying. Or they're fooling themselves. Kid McCoy, for example, had lots of regrets. One time he was keeping a wealthy widow on the string and she was found dead. He served a seven year rap for that. Seven years and three months. And still he came back. But he didn't come back far enough. After seven years and three months, does anybody ever come back far enough?

For those who care enough Kid McCoy's suicide note reads:

To Whom It May Concern: For the past eight years I have wanted to help humanity especially the youngsters who do not know nature's laws. That is the proper carriage of the body or the right way to eat, etc.

Everything in my possession I want to go the my dear wife Sue E. Selby. To all my dear friends, I wish you the best of luck. Sorry I could not endure the world's madness. The best to all.

Norman Selby
P.S. In my pocket you will find $17.75.

Dempster was the cop assigned to the case. I asked him if he found the $17.75 in Selby's pocket. He said

Yeah. He had. Seventeen dollars is not too much to go out of the world with, I told him. You're right about that, Dempster said. Lack of money was one thing Dempster understood. He had five kids at home and a sixth in the oven. I had no kids at home and none on the way. If there was one thing I agreed with McCoy about it was the madness of the world. It got to him a lot sooner that it got to me. Now it's getting to me good. The real question of living is how much madness we endure?

"Someday I'm just going to climb out on the window ledge and cry out all the burdens of my heart," Dempster said. He was forty-five years old with a ruddy complexion and puffy eyes. But he was a good man to have on the case. He was popular with the press and he was a boxing fan.

He could have been a boxer himself. He had the build for it.

Taller and broader than McCoy.

Did you ever see Selby fight?" I asked him.

"Lots of times."

"Was he any good?"

"Better than most." Dempster said. He offered me a stick of gum, but I refused. Dempster chewed gum instead of smoking. As far as I knew he was the only cop in Detroit who didn't smoke. Detroit that year was driving everybody to smoking, to drinking, or to committing suicide. Or maybe it just wasn't Detroit, maybe it was something else. Nazi marching songs were big that year.

"He was the real McCoy," he said.

"That's where the expression comes from?"

Dempster shrugged and went back to the elevators. "I leave it to you college hotshots to know that stuff. I'm lucky to know where my prick is."

When I thought about all those mouths he had to feed, he should have kept it where it was.

Later, after the body had been removed and the photographers had dropped their used flashbulbs all over the lobby, Dempster, even though he was off-duty, came back down, and I bought him a drink. It's always good to keep on the good side of the cops. I also had the feeling he needed an excuse not to rush home.

"You know the worse thing about a suicide?" Dempster asked.

"What?" I said. I noticed that when he picked up his bottle of beer that his hands were shaking.

"It's calling the wife or the husband or the parents. That's the part I hate."

"How did she take it?"

"How would you take it?"

"Lousy," I said. "It hurts like hell."

"Well, that's how she took it. I don't think he left her a lot either. And what's that stuff about nature's laws? Do you know anything about nature's laws?"

"We try to kill our enemies and love our friends," I told him. "That's the only law I know. That and the fact that the Tigers aren't going to win the pennant."

"That guy had everything and he goes and does himself in."

"I don't think he had everything."

"Kept a lot of good-looking women on the string. That's enough."

"I got a good looking woman myself," I said. "And one's plenty. Actually, one is more than plenty." Around Dempster I wanted to appear to be more sophisticated than I really was. In point of fact, Brahms' Fourth Symphony, with its mirror fugue, possessed far more ideas than I would ever have in my entire life. There! I've gone and said it.

"Then why don't you go home to her?"

"That's a good question," I said. "Why don't I go home to her?" It was then I remembered the music cabinet. All the problems caused by Kid McCoy had caused me to forget about the surprise.

"Why are you unhappy all the time?" Dempster asked. "You always look as if somebody was getting ready to run you over with a steam-roller."

"You don't see me all the time," I told him.

He stood up and winked. "I guess that's what makes my day," he said. "See you the next time someone does himself in." He was a big guy and when he walked out of the bar he ambled like a bear. I liked him. He was older than I was and he knew a lot more. Chalk marks on the pavement knew a lot more than I ever would. Especially about women.

When I drove home, I noticed that the lights in the apartment were not on. It was eleven-thirty and Tobey still wasn't home. Maybe she had a late rehearsal. She had been having a lot of late rehearsals. I kept coming home to a dark apartment and I was getting tired of it. No one wants to be the first one home all the time. I decided to wait in the car. I turned on some music and waited. No matter where you find yourself in life, someone is always singing a song. Sad ones. Slow ones. Fast ones. My wife loved classical music, but I didn't know very much about it. Except for Brahms' Fourth Symphony. I listened to that every chance I had. Because I was usually focused on something else, I just didn't have that many chances to listen to classical music. To reduce my anger, I turned up the radio. Where was Jimmy Durante when I needed him? Some scholar said Durante was a descendant of Dante. I said that with Hitler on the horizon we're all descendants of Dante's Inferno.

"Shut the goddamn music off," one of my neighbors shouted. Our neighbors were always shouting about one thing or another. It kept their minds of themselves.

"Sorry," I said. I didn't realize how late it really was or how loud the music was. So I shut off the music and sat in silence. Along about midnight a cab pulled up and my wife got out. I stayed in my car and watched her. She paid the driver and entered the apartment. I waited for the lights to go on. Waited for her to find the music cabinet. Twenty minutes passed. Time, I thought. HURRY UP PLEASE. IT'S TIME.

As I walked up the stairs, she was coming down. She was carrying a suitcase. She was wearing a white dress with red flowers on it. Her light brown hair was pulled back tight and looked as it fit had just been washed.

"What's going on?" I asked.

"What does it look like," she said. "I'm moving out. I'll come back for the rest of my stuff later."

"What do you mean you're moving out?" I asked her. We were standing in the middle of the third floor landing and I could hear everybody in the world waking up.

"What do you think it means?" she asked. "It means I'm moving out. I'm leaving."

"Quit answering my questions with questions," I

told her, "Let's go upstairs and talk about it."

"I don't want to go upstairs," she said.

I reached for the suitcase, but Tobey pulled away. "Don't touch me."

"I'm not touching you." I told her. I felt as if someone had taken a razor, cut my skin, and pulled me out naked. I started to cry, "Why are you doing this?" I asked.

"Oh for God's sakes," she said.

"It's too late to go out." I told her. "At least wait until morning."

"I don't want to wait until morning."

For the sake of the neighbors, we were trying to keep our voices down.

I reached for the suitcase again, but she pulled it away.

She was a tall woman, taller than me, with long brown hair and grey eyes. Slender. Sometimes she looked so beautiful I could die, but then I had always been a sucker for good looking women who were smart and who possessed lively spirits. She was getting ready to hit me with the suitcase. The way she was holding it, thrusting it toward my face and chest there couldn't have been too much in it. "Can't we just talk about it in our own apartment," I pleaded. She wasn't crying. She wasn't crying at all.

"No," she said. "There isn't anything to talk about."

"We've been married four years. There ought to be something to say."

"There is," she nodded. Her lower lip was trembling. "But not now."

"Yes, now," I said. Every cell in my body said now.

The buttons on my coat said now. The lights on the stairway said now. The dead man in the hotel room said now. My conversation with Dempster said now. My shoelaces said now. The beating of my heart said now. I grabbed her wrist and started to twist it, "Come upstairs and we'll talk." Blood pumping in and out said now. My whole life said *now*.

"Get out of my way!"

"Didn't you see the music cabinet?" I asked her. I more than asked her.

"You're hurting me!"

"You're hurting me!"

"It's somebody else?" I asked. I more than asked her.

"No," she said.

I sat down on the stairs, collapsed to the stairs really, and now I was sobbing so violently I thought I was going to throw up.

"For God's sakes," she said. "That's what I can't stand. I don't want to hurt you, but I have to go. I made up my mind before I came home."

"Come upstairs," I pleaded. "I got you a music cabinet, goddamn it. I bought you a music cabinet. Doesn't that mean anything?"

"Yes," she said. "It means something." In spite of everything, her voice retained its essential music. She was from North Carolina and had a southern accent tinged with Elizabethan cadences. I had loved the essential music of her from the very first.

"Where are you going? I have the right to know. Who is he? I have the right to know."

She had held forth her hand to touch me on the

shoulder, to steady me, but now she pulled it back.

"Please, Sam, I don't want to hurt you," she said. "I'll call you in the morning. First thing in the morning."

"But I bought you the music cabinet," I pleaded, but she had picked up her suitcase. "I bought you the music cabinet." She started down the stairs." She didn't turn around, so I shouted at her back, her long brown hair swinging angrily back and forth, pulled by some great invisible bell-puller. "I you leave me," I shouted. "I'll kill myself. I swear it!"

A man's voice boomed forth from one of the apartments. "So go kill yourself. Just do it in peace and quiet, why don't you?"

"Shut up, Homer," the woman in 3-D shouted back at him. What in the hell is going on, I thought. I didn't understand anything. My chest was so tight I thought I was dying of a heart attack.

A door to another apartment opened a crack and a short, gray-haired woman stuck her face out. I was a fool in her eyes. I was a fool in everybody's eyes. I had forgotten the proper carriage of my body. My body, in fact, was trembling and I wanted to throw up. Not the beer. Not the food. I wanted to throw up my whole life. I wanted to go to sleep and I wanted to go downstairs. I wanted to find my wife's lover and batter him until his eyes popped out of his head. I wanted to kill him. I wanted to kill myself. I wanted to kill somebody. I wanted to take a baseball bat and break all the glass in the world. I wanted to call my friend Dempster and throw myself at his mercy. I wanted to pray to God. I wanted there to be a God to pray to. I wanted the neighbors to mind their own businesses. I wanted to float into bed. I wanted Tobey to run up the stairs and back into my arms. I wanted to stop crying. I wanted to catch my breath. I wanted to fall asleep and dream. I wanted good dreams. I wanted to hear the bell and come out fighting. I wanted to rape her. I wanted to go home to my parents. I wanted to crawl into the womb. I wanted. I wanted. I wanted.

"Are you alright?" the woman asked, not daring to push the door open any wider.

I shook my head. I nodded.

"You want me to call the cops?"

I blew the bad air out of my body. I shook my head. "I've seen enough cops for one day." I grasped the railing and managed to stand up. I dragged myself back upstairs.

"Happy Easter," the woman called behind me. I stopped and waited to hear her door close. And then I went upstairs and bound my own apartment. When I went inside, the cabinet was still in the living-room, but it didn't look the same. It looked smaller and dirtier. There were a chips and dents and spots that had been poorly retouched I hadn't noticed before. The note I had written to Tobey had fallen to the floor. I picked it up and placed it on top of the cabinet. After a half hour or so I went into Tobey's closet and I gathered together as much of my wife's music as I could find. I tore the sheets in half, into quarters, in eighths. I tossed the papers into the bathtub and set fire to them. Beethoven, Mozart, and Brahms would die for her sins.

The flames shot up and so I turned the shower on it to keep the fire from getting out of hand.

Scarlett O'Hara could cry out, "Tomorrow is

another day." But there was nothing in my soul that could do that.

Christ! I had never seen such a mess.

Scarlett might vow "I'll never go hungry again." I lay down on the tile floor next to the bathtub. The smellof burnt music was foul, smelled worse than Kid McCoy'shotel room. I placed a wet towel over my face. To hell with Nature's Laws and correct posture. I had the distinct feeling I was going to be lonely for a very long time.

SHAME

The unraveling of his marriage had started simply enough. His wife had left their Detroit apartment to go out for a walk. When she hadn't returned in a half-hour, he went downstairs and found her in a phone booth talking to someone. As soon as he opened the door, she hung up. Why did she have to leave the house to call someone?, he asked. She offered no explanation, no plausible explanation that is. Talking with her was like reading an article on dairy farming and you had no idea why you were reading it and you had very little idea what the writers were talking about. She said was calling a friend to check about a rehearsal schedule. I didn't believe her.

Not for one minute.

Somebody had to be blown up in the first scene and then put together in the last. That was the movie formula. But Samuel Matson, peering into the shambles of his 50 year old life, had come up with a secondary formula. One not so commercial. And the formula had the musty smell of philosophy behind it. Tell me what you are ashamed of, and I shall tell you who you are.

2

Did you ever see a man take out his glass eye and hold it in the palm of his hand as if it were hard candy? It is tosay the least discomfiting to see, but after the atrocitiesapproved by King Leopold, atrocities committed in theBelgian Congo, after the exterminations of the

Armenians, after the Holocaust, after the starvation of millions in Stalin's Russia, after the constant repetition of the word *Genocide*, it is as if Humanity had blinded itself or as if we were walking around with glass eyes. We shall be like the blind Gloucester in King Lear and go about the world feelingly…or more accurately, unfeelingly.

Samuel unfeelingly removed the photo of his ex-wife out of the bottom of the fourth drawer of the green bureau in his bedroom, the photo in the silver frame in the very bottom of the bottom under the autographed photos of movie stars and *National Geographics* discovering what lands that were left to be discovered and wrapped it carefully in old newspaper. The newspaper and the photo smelled of past lives in Detroit andelsewhere. Here, there, and everywhere. Here, there, and nowhere at all.

The snapshot showed Tobey with her arms around the neck of her father, with Tobey's mother hovering in the background. Samuel had taken the picture a long time ago, and now he thought the old man, as he lay recovering from heart surgery might find some comfort in it.

The front page of the newspaper that he used for wrapping paper held forth with a story about a Rajah who had spent his entire life trying to prove that he was alive.

RAJAH DIES AFTER WINNING 25 YEAR FIGHT TO PROVE THAT HE WAS ALIVE

An Exchange Telegraph Agency dispatch from Calcutta said that Ramendra Narayan Roy, Rajah of Bhowal, who won a 25 year fight in the courts last week to prove hewas legally alive, died Saturday in Calcutta while waitingfor King George VI to sign an order restoring his vastdomain.

The Privy Council, highest judicial authority in the British Empire, last Tuesday recognized the Rajah's claim by dismissing the case of Ranee Bighabati, 'widow' of the Rajah, who said that Roy died at Darjeeling in 1909 andwas cremated.

The Rajah maintained that while his funeral pyre wasburning, a heavy downpour revived him. He said he was rescued by passing beggars with whom he lived for 12 years while suffering loss of memory.

How fitting that we should spend our lives proving the obvious, trying to prove that we are still alive. Or is it so obvious? Someday, Samuel thought, he would make a story from it. Unfortunately, the idea would not make anyone hear cash registers ring. Cash registers ringing, the symphonic instruments for the modern world. Adagio for plugged nickels; sonata for dollars. A penny for your thoughts. More than I am getting now.

If Samuel could find the door to the big dream and open it. Walk through it. Walk away from everything and everyone. Defeat River was only a hop, skip, and a jump away. From henceforth Samuel promised himself that he would write only about the dead coming back to life.

The world, of course, was filled to overflowing with stories.

Rajahs and suicides and soccer scores. That was mostly what the world was. A repository of beginnings, middles, and ends.

3

Another story about the dead coming back to life is this:

The Fish and Game Club. That's what the sign said. But it wasn't a fish and Game Club. It was a front for the KKK. Samuel knew it.

Samuel had done research on the Klan, and after some southern newspapers picked up his articles It did not make him loved.

In the 1930s & 40s Tobey's father Kenneth owned and operated a cafe in Shallow's Ford, and the Klan, learning that Samuel was actually in their midst, had burned a cross on Kenneth's front lawn. In theory, a burning cross should not be frightening; in reality, a burning cross is very frightening. Fear shoes the mare.

Tobey's father and mother, and Tobey's younger sister Janet lay together on the floor of the master bedroom, lay between the twin beds in case someone started shooting. Just because a cross was burning, it did not mean that there would be no shooting. Kenneth kept this rifle under his left hand, just in itcame to shooting.

What was the name of the cafe, Samuel wondered. It was strange he could not remember the name of a place that he sat in so many times. You grow older and so many names get erased. You grow older and much of your life gets erased.

Samuel thought: I should have helped Kenneth in the cafe. He needed help. But Samuel wanted to prove to Tobey's parents, to the world, and not lastly to himself that he had his own profession. Now he could barely remember what that profession was, buried as it was in the fourth drawer of a green bureau. When Lee, Tobey's mother, suggested that he move his typewriter and papers from the living room table to a card table set up in the basement, Samuel took the suggestion as a criticism of who he was or wanted to be. He would not be moved easily.

But hadn't he caused enough trouble? Wasn't it Samuel's articles on the Klan that caused the men and women and indeed some children in white hoods to turn out in force, even though the Cafe employed only two Negroes. Maybe he shouldn't go back to Shallow Ford, should not go at all. Turning up in person after so many years would stir up too many sad memories and the old man didn't need more sadness in his life. Who does?

Yes, Samuel thought. Perhaps he should just mail the snapshot and be done with it. As much as anything in your past is done with.

4

And then there was Ruby's daughter. Ruby's daughter—she had a name, but Samuel remembered her only as Ruby's daughter (You grow older and so many names get erased)—worked at the Cafe on the main street of town. Dressed in a plain white uniform, the same costume she wore every day, she was the thinnest girl Samuel had ever seen, with straight brown hair, under a hairnet when she served food, and blue eyes with all the brightness washed out of them. Legs and arms like sticks,

And no breasts to speak off, but capable of falling in love.Worthy of being loved. Shy. If you looked at her straight in the face, you feared she might turn and run away.

Ruby's daughter was in love with a man in Virginia who owned a garage and repaired motorcycles, a man who was thirty -seven or thirty-eight, nearly twenty years older than Ruby's daughter.

An age difference that Ruby would not allow her daughter to forget.

Ruby's fiancé' (if that is the correct term) had moved from Shallow seven months earlier to Virginia to open a garage with his older brother.

Ruby's daughter wanted to marry him as soon as she gets away from the café and helping her mother. It wasn't just the ticket for the bus she needed. She needed to overcome the fear of leaving behind a life she knew. She had to be sure that the man really wanted her. How humiliating it would be if she had to return home, heartbroken. If she returned pregnant, she would by covered with shame.

She and Ruby got up every morning at three-thirty to be in the kitchen of the Cafe by five. The Cafe served breakfast at five thirty.

The once married man in question had sent Ruby's daughter a snapshot of himself. He was in his blue mechanic's uniform and he was standing in front of the Bus Stop Garage. He was not smiling and he clutched a rag covered with oil. He was as thin as Ruby's Daughter. Samuel thought they were meant for one another. Between them they would produce the thinnest children on the planet.

But how could anyone know who was meant for whom.

5

I am ashamed of not having enough money, Samuel thought. Tobey had been correct in leaving him. She could see the writing on the wall, when Samuel couldn't even find the wall. Back to the wall. What a metaphor that was. Need a Hebrew prophet to read the writing on the wall.

I don't have any money Samuel thought. I am going to have to declare myself a building and sell air-rights. In America, buildings are treated better than people anyway. Or perhaps that is true the world over. Perhaps I shall be a skyscraper, but one that never casts a shadow. Casting shadows frequently causes trouble. Perhaps that is why so many people, such as Ruby's daughter, try to go through life without casting a shadow.

But it's strange, Samuel thought, what I am most ashamed of. Was all clear to him. Perhaps Tobey had explained, or subsequent events had explained themselves. Even without historians, history has ways of working itself out.

THINKS WIFE WITH ANOTHER, SHOOTS WOMAN, KILLS SELF

How many times, Samuel wondered, had he actually thought about suicide? A hundred? A thousand? Every other moment of every day?

And for what?

No matter how often he thought about taking his own life, he was not ashamed of such thoughts. Who in his right mind would never consider opening that door?

6

The comedian on the radio said: "I thought my wife and I had a good marriage, but when we moved from California toMassachusetts, I noticed that we had the same milkman.
Ha. Ha. Has. Ha. Ha. Ha. Ha. Ha.

7

Samuel was lost. He had gotten off at the wrong exit, been driving around for twenty minutes and for the life of him he couldn't remember where he was going. It was strange. Everything had changed. Nothing was the way it was. The newscaster on the car radio said:

James Bosley, 23, of West Conshohocken, last night shot and seriously wounded Mrs. Mary Quioiser of this borough, and then killed himself. He mistook Mrs. Quoiser for his wife of three weeks and thought she was with another man.

The radio snapped, popped, crackled with improbabilities. Turning back toward the highway leading out of town, Samuel listened for a follow-up to the news-story but there wasn't any.

Sometimes the story alone is not enough. There has to be a follow up.

The photograph of Tobey and her parents lay on the seat of the Buick. Gotten off at the wrong exit. How Freudian can you get? The county hospital where his ex-father-in-law was recovering from heart surgery shouldn't be that difficult to locate. He changed channels just in time to catch the last two minutes of Debby Boone singing "You Light Up My Life." Yeah. Yeah.

My life was so lit up it was burning like that cross burning on Kenneth's front lawn.

8

Lost. How many times had he been lost in his life? Once when he had gone looking for Tobey when Tobey had fallen in love with somebody else. Or fallen in lust. Whatever it was. Everybody was much younger then and their bodies spun out different tales.

And then there was the incident with Ruby's daughter:

Idiotic, Samuel thought, when Ruby's daughter said to him, "The people in town would talk if they saw the two of us walking out together."

"Walking out?" Samuel said. "I'm just going to take your picture. So you can send it to Willis. You said you didn't have a picture to send your boyfriend."

He was looking for a suitable backdrop for the snapshot. It would have been much easier simply to take the picture inside the café, but Samuel wanted something more artistic, something to make her fiancée' sit up and take notice.

"I know." Ruby's daughter blushed. "But I didn't think it meant us walking out together." She looked around nervously. There was no one on the sidewalk. They had crossed to a stone wall by the cemetery and then to a wall of red clay. Authentic southern red clay.

The red clay would make a suitable backdrop for a color shot. His entire life would make a suitable backdrop. Ruby's daughter walked quickly. She just wanted to get the whole thing over with. When I think of the skin of Ruby's daughter I think of the clay, her skin's reddish tint. She was chameleon-like. Her skin took on the color of whatever place she was.

Perhaps he had been wrong in suggesting the project. He just thought he was helping her. Or maybe he should be afraid of Klansmen driving by to get him. There was always something to be afraid of. Ruby's daughter was ready to bolt and run. I had brought her a moral problem that I had not anticipated. No good deed goes unpunished.

She was shivering. Not from the cold. She looked up and down the deserted streets. If anybody had seen herwalking around, she would most likely bolt and run.

"People will think I'm trying to steal you away from Tobey," Ruby's daughter said quickly, turning her face away from him. "That's how people think in this town." She was only eighteen, and had never been away from home. Sweet. Innocent. But she knew the people of the town. The good Christians who were also members of the Klan and who attended church every Sunday to preserve their immortal souls.

"I don't care how people think in this town," Samuel declared.

"Yes," she said, not looking at him, standing straight and stiff in front of the clay pile. "But I have to live here." She refused to smile. Shifting her weight from one foot to the other.

Samuel took two or three quick snapshots. No way he could get her to relax. She seemed to be apologizing for everything in her life. For the strangers who were out to harm him. Or townsfolk who were angry at Tobey for marrying a northernerwho wrote articles for newspapers.

One who didn't understand God's laws about segregation. Ruby's daughter practically ran back to the café. To prevent her further embarrassment, Samuel remained behind, standing like a stone wall behind the cemetery's stone wall. After a half hour passed, he walked slowly back to the café and was treated to a coke and pieces of Ruby's justly famous peach cobbler.

When Samuel mailed Ruby's daughter the snapshots from Manhattan, a few 3 by 5s. She never wrote back herself. Ruby's daughter thanked him through Tobey's parents. Samuel imagined that she had sent the pictures to her boyfriend in the Virginia garage, but he never did find out what had happened after that.

Did he Willis fall in love with her because of the picture? Did they get married? Did he ask her "Who took those photos? And then what did you two do?" Did he imagine that we were really walking out together and that she tried to pry me away from Tobey when we were newly married.Photos get blown up. Lives too get blown out of proportion. Blown apart and never put back together again.

9

Samuel, singing along with Sinatra all of a sudden started to think about Alexander J. Dorogokuptz? I was the kid who pelted Sinatra with eggs when the Chairman of the Board played Radio City Music Hall. Later, days later, years later, was

Alexander ever ashamed of what he did? So he ended up as a footnote in some biography? What did the guy do with the rest of his life? Did he brag about throwing the eggs to get women into bed with him? Stopped at a gas station to ask for directions, but directions to where?

Samuel was beginning to feel atightness in his chest and was finding it increasingly difficult to breathe. The past weighed too heavily upon his soul. That is if there was such a substance as soul. Or, like the past itself, a non-substance.

When he stepped out of his car, he was already babbling about Dorogoputz and Sinatra and Debby Boone. "What about Sinatra getting pelted with eggs at Radio City. What do you think about some idiot doing that?", he asked the six-foot black man walking toward the pump.

"What, sir?"

"Sinatra the way he sings. You like his songs?"

"You want gas?"

"It is all in the phrasing. He's got so many great songs."

The gas station attendant pulled out a red kerchief out of his pocket, wiped his brow, and scratched his head.

"Leaded? Unleaded?"

"Everything that matters in the universe is in the phrasing. Ripeness is all. But so is phrasing." Samuel could hear with horror the babble pouring out of his mouth. His dry mouth.

The black man nodded, pulled down some paper towelsand wiped his large hands with them.

"You want me to pump gas?"

"Sorry. I am trying to find the County Hospital. Am I on the right road?" Samuel finally noticed that the gas station worker had his name stitched in blue thread across the pocket of his grease-stained short-sleeved green shirt. Gus. His name was Gus.

Gus wadded the dirty papers into a ball and tossed them into the trash barrel next to the pump.

"Sorry, sir. I have no idea."

"A friend of mine is dying. Just tell me how to get there."

"I don't know. There's a phone book in the office. If you want to look it, help yourself. It's cooler inside." Gus turned and walked back to the office. There was no one else inside.

Samuel spread out his two arms palm up, as if to ask, 'what's going on here?'

Gus stood behind the glass door, folded his arms, and stared out at Samuel. Samuel felt foolish. He should never have gotten carried away about Sinatra and rotten eggs.

"Aren't you even going to pump my gas?" he asked.

As if he didn't hear him, Gus turned away from the door and sat down behind a large oak desk.

Samuel climbed back into his car. "Take your leaded gas nozzle and stick it up your leaded ass," he mumbled to himself.

At a second near-by station, Samuel kept his commentsto himself. He only asked for gas and directions.

10

Across the street from the hospital there were two baseball fields, each immaculately cared for, complete with green wooden fences to hit home-runs over. The grass too was bright green in the afternoon sunshine. Not at all like the fields in the poorer neighborhoods of New York, where there was broken glass between the tattered bases, and nothing cared for. If there had been rain the day before, puddles would dominate the infields and outfields because there was no drainage. Drainage, Samuel concluded, was important for ball fields and the human body.

But these fields across from the county hospital, where his ex-father-in-law lay dying—well they presented two good reasons parents uprooted their familes and moved to the country. There were five boys, three whites and two blacks, playing hit and catch. Samuel estimated that the boys were eleven, twelve, thirteen at most. The baseball rose in a high arc and the second baseman ran out to short center field and the ball settled into his glove.

Samuel parked his car, removed his sports coat, laid it on the passenger's side of the front seat. Damn, he thought. I should have brought y baseball glove with me. Never go anywhere without our baseball glove. Isn't that one of the more important rules of growing up? That, and keep track of the drainage. He stepped out of the car and walk to out to wherethe boys were hitting and fielding.

He stood and watched for awhile. No other grown-ups around. Finally he approached the black boy in the batter's box.

The boy tossed a ball up and hit a grounder to the outfield.

Samuel stopped next to the batter and fielded the ball when one of the outfielders tossed it in.

"Hey, man, whtja doing?"

124

The batter was tall and lean, like a young Satchel Paige. Oh, Satchel what a pitcher. With the slowest walk from the bullpen to the pitcher's mound in the history of the game. "Can I hit some to you guys?"

"Naah. We like hitting ourselves." The other boys ran in to see what Samuel was up to? Was he trying to push them off the field for some little league team?

Samuel removed his wallet and extracted twenty-fivedollars. The boys' eyes widened. "I'll pay you each for rentingthe bat and ball. I'll hit you some long fly balls for twenty minutes or so. Then you can continue your game. How's thatfor a good deal?"

"Let the man hit some," the other black boy said. "I can use some of that." He was playing in his bare feet.

An agreement was reached. A white boy with blonde hair and a New York Yankees cap took the money. He stuffed into his pants back pocket and ran out to the field.

"You don't look like you're dressed for baseball,"the batter said, handing over his bat.

"No," Samuel said. "I'm not dressed for anything."

A white boy with his blue baseball cap turned backwardasked, "Do you want me to pitch to you?"

"No. I'll just toss the ball up and hit it. Get back. Getway back." Hit a home run for his ex-father-in-law he thought.

The old man learning how humiliating it is to grow old. Perhaps Kenneth or one of his daughters would be looking out the window toward the field. It was baseball. The wind was blowing out. The grass on the fields had been freshly mowed. The smell of it filled his nostrils. He had almost forgotten what that meant.

Dead grass lay unraked upon the living grass. The fields smelled of past lives, with the six of them in the afternoon sun pursuing one lesser kind of happiness.

Samuel tossed the ball into the air, swung and missed. He picked it up and tried again. Two. Three. Four times. A sign on the outfield fence where the scrawny black kid had posted himself advertised pizza at some local take-out place. Samuel felt hungry. He was in need of a good meal and a good night's sleep. Find a motel somewhere.

"Come on, mistah, hit one," the left fielder called. All the fielders looked so far away. And the bat was too small and too light for him. He swung and the ball rolled slowly up the third base line. The boy with the backward blue baseball cap grabbedit and tossed it back. Samuel caught it on the fly. He just needed another 25 years to prove he was alive. The boy shook his head.

Disappointed, Samuel guessed. He promised them high fly balls. Too late in life to become a baseball player. Too late in life to become much of anything. He tossed, swung, hit a fly to the center fielder. He became afraid of all the unresolved conflicts that had built up over the years. The ball was tossed back to him and Samuel swung viciously at it and it hit thebottom of the center field with a hard dull thud.

"Good one, mistah."

No, Samuel thought. Not great. He turned his glance away from the ball field to the immense county hospital, its windows gleaming in the sun. In a few more minutes I shall go inside ad drop off the photo in its silver frame, just leave it with one of thenurses. No note. No nothing. Just a snapshot really. Tobey would know who it was for.

GIFTS

Doctor Rosemont should not have stopped at his parents' graves, but with the doctor's wife and twenty-five year old daughter crying day and night, staying at home was no longer such a pleasant option. In addition, the good doctor had promised to visit Buzz's asthmatic son and provide a shot of adrenalin. The Donora Cemetery was on the way to the farm. He wasn't going out of his way at all, although the smog was making the familiar roads more difficult to find.

Adding promise to promise, the Doctor had promised his secretary that he would return by 3. Before he walked down the stairs of his office building, he called the hospital at Charleroi (there was no hospital in Donora proper) and asked an acquaintance who worked the admissions' desk to keep track of male patients with red hair. Especially any new person not living in the area.

The Doctor's drive out of town was slow and somewhat disconcerting because smog had settled heavily upon the township. It certainly was not the first time that Donora breathed uneasily under a cover of fog and smoke and zinc and God knows what else. Topography was partly to blame. Surrounded by clusters of hills and high bluffs, there was not enough winds to dissipate the chemical fumes. Coal barges on the river and the smoke stacks if the Steel and Wire Plant owned by the U.S. Steel Corporation had been completely obscured. Whenever the coal barges made their journey to Pittsburgh, women ran out to take in their laundry from the clotheslines. Even the most religious among them cursed that dust.

By the time he reached the dirt lane leading into the cemetery, the Doctor had concluded that the dead were lucky, They did not have breathe dirty air, though perhaps they breathed in other ways, In addition, the Dead took up too much living space. Dreaming space. Mental space. Spiritual space. Parents. Friends. Relatives. Soldiers (It was three years since V-J Day). The dead frequently crowded out the living as they came from beyond bearing the gifts of memory. *"It was suffering and incapacity that created all afterworlds."* As for God, well he hadn't made up his mind about that. Try as he might, there was no way to shake off his depressing thoughts. Hell-bent.

How does the Lion become a child? Damn it! He had a right to his depression. His doctor's oath was to do no harm, but—well, he was now hell-bent upon killing someone if he could only locate the man who had changed his daughter's life for the worse. *How does a child become a man and the man become a Lion?* Kill the man who had hurt his only child, even if it meant spending eternity in Hell. If there were a Hell, it most likely could not be more dismal than the landscape he found himself in day after day. He should have moved away years ago. Afterworlds indeed.

Did not Zarathusa speak: *"A little revenge is more human than revenge."* But was it not also true that Tragedy did not exist in the singular? Tragedies occurred always in the plural. No tragedy ever visited just one person and person alone. The effects of tragedies rippled out and then further out until innumerable souls were touched. Strange to be a doctor and think so much about souls, when he was entrusted only with the housing. He couldn't help himself. He was no longer making sense to himself. His best thoughts were being choked to death.

Carbon monoxide in the air was befuddling him, causing him to make bad judgments. Driving out to Buzz's farm now seemedto him a bad judgment. Bad judgment, indeed.

The graves that abutted Buzz's farm were not well-kept. That was the bad-taste joke all the time he and Buzz were growing up—when Buzz's parents died, all Buzz would have to do is toss their bodies from their second floor window, and they would fall where they needed to be. Thus, it came to pass that his high-school buddy's parents did land in the cemetery, side by side, in Washington County for Eternity. As if anybody needed to be in Donora ("Next to Yours, the Best Town in the U.S.A.—Population 14,000) "—how about that for public relations illusion?) when the smog was upon it—which was becoming more frequent. Sulfur and Stan Musial. That's what Donora had to brag about, although this late October Day made the atmosphere spongy, sodden, more smothering than it had ever had been in years.

The doctor sniffed sulfur dioxide in the air, and walked past two pick-up trucks rusting in Buzz's backyard. A German shepherd barked. If the smokestacks from the foundries, coke plants and zinc furnaces were not good for the lungs of human beings, they were perhaps more harmful to small animals, Driving oh so cautiously from Donora to Buzz's farm, The doctor had seen a dead collie on the road and there had been two dead cats in the cemetery, As for people, well his secretary had said that Ralph Schwerer, the undertaker had already been called out to collect three bodies.

The doctor wondered if the annual football game between the Donora and Monongahela high schools, to be played on Saturday, would have to be called off. Who would be able to see it?

That would be a shame because Donora had some first class seniors and was heavily favored, but if the smog did not dissipateby game time, it could well reach toxic level, Soon the offices of the seven other doctors in town would be crowded with the old and the very young, with those suffering from headaches and abdominal pain. Many would be confined to their homes by vomiting and who knows how many of his patients would be coughing up blood?An entire town huddling under smoke trees and suffering battle fatigue, with the closest hospital miles away in Charleroi.

2

Buzz. Once the field he was driving past was filled with bees. *Buzz. Buzz. Buzz.* In fact that was how Jamie received the nickname. His great-grandfather had been a bee-keeper and for a time Jamie thought of keeping bees himself, but that was before Zinc and Sulphur Acid Plant had opened its doors and invited the citizens in to earn their keep. The honey stomach of the world lay elsewhere. Now the local joke was bees would have to cross the Monongehela River and fly north, past Pittsburgh, perhaps fly all the way to the Canadian border to find enough flowers to pollinate. Maybe that would be the fate of the human race: to build factory after belching factory, making it impossible for bees to survive, and if bees died, they would most likely drag the human race with it.

The doctor lit his second cigarette of the day, but like the first, it did not taste right. Cigarettes had not tasted right for days, Good ole Stan Musial. Weren't he and Williams doing ads for Chesterfields? He flicked the cigarette into the mud, straightened his tie, and grabbed his black bag. If sulfur dioxide didn't kill the bees, then the mites would. Always something coming at you from one direction or another. You wake up every morning, but you can't see what's coming.

Buzz stepped out of he door and waved a kerosene lantern back and forth. "That you, Howard?"

"It's me, Buzz."

Buzz apologized for dragging the doctor out to the farm, but Dr. Rosemont waved him away, climbed the stairs with its threadbare green carpet to the son's bedroom and administered a dose of aminophyllis. The smog was particularly threatening to persons suffering from Asthma. Buzz's son—Billy—was in his early forties and lived at home, helping Buzz with the livestock. Billy's age and asthma condition had kept him out of the war. So maybe there was a touch of irony there. What kept him sick possibly had saved his life.

Buzz had a second, younger son—Barton—who was now in New York with a small role in *Rigaletto* at the Met. The Doctor's daughter, Sandra, had been planning to take a package from Buzz to the big city for Bart, but now that was not going to happen.

No, it wasn't going to happen at all.

At one time it seemed as if Barton and Sandra would marry, but that didn't happen either. Buzz's obsession with Sandra didn't help the courtship. Not at all.

By the time the Doctor came downstairs, Buzz was seated in the kitchen. The brown-paper package of wool shirts for Bartonsat on the table. The package, awkwardly wrapped was tied with white string.

"Coffee, Doc?"

"No, thanks Buzz. Coffee doesn't taste good to me today."

"Me neither." Buzz was a scarecrow of a man, six feet of tough, browned, wrinkled hide, topped by a head of thin white hair. He and Doc Rosemont had been friends for over 40 years, though there were a few years of a terrible falling out when it was becoming obvious that Buzz had shown a romantic yearning for the Doctor's daughter and being together was just too awkward, The old fool. Couldn't he see he was much too old for her. For him there would not be any jitterbugging at the Savoy. Of course, Buzz never acted on his yearnings because he wasn't that kind of man and there was the problem of Barton. What idiots old men can be.

"Billy gonna be okay?"

"Yeah. Just look in on him every fifteen minutes or so. If he has trouble breathing, you're gonna have to go to Charleroi, There's no way I'm going to make it back out here until the fog lifts."

"You think it's the smoke from the Zinc factory? Eh?"

The Doctor shrugged. He dealt with respiratory disorders, so Donora gave him plenty of work, lots of things to think about, The older you get, the more difficult it becomes to breathe, because so much of the past weighs upon you like a heavy blanket of fog and smoke. Until, of course, you stopped breathing all

133

together. And then what? *Buzz buzz.*

Was that he sound of Eternity?

"Did you have your radio on? You hear what happened out on the highway?" Buzz asked, He waved Howard to a kitchen chair, but the Doctor, pulling on his gloves, remained standing.

"No. I had to concentrate on my driving. The smog is getting too thick. So I have to turn around right away, or I'll be stuck out here and I got patients waiting for me."

"Hell, I've been stuck out here all my life," Buzz said, turning to the kitchen table to fetch the package. "My parents did me no favors leaving me this place."

"Can I use your phone? I need to call my office."

"Sure, Doc. You know where it is."

Buzz was right about that. The phone was on a small tablein the narrow hallway leading from the kitchen to the living-room.

It had been there for years. As he talked, he studied the large upholstered chair in the living-room where Buzz's father say night after night, reading the paper and shaking his head. "What is the world coming to?" the old man would ask. "What is the world coming to?"

Buzz's father was a strange one all right. He was fascinated by spiritualism and table-tipping. One night, the table upon the telephone now stood was used in an experiment and the table rose six inches off the floor. Franklin was mad as a hornet when he discovered that Buzz and Howard had played a trick on him. Not as if spiritualism wasn't playing tricks on everyone. As if coming back from the dead was what the Dead wanted. What was needed was for his daughter to come back from life.

Carol, the Doctor's assistant, said that the office was crowded and that he should get back right away, that the Halloween Parade was marching down Main Street because she could hear the music, but that she couldn't see a thing out of the office windows. People with handkerchiefs tied over their faces were staggering in from Main Street, with everybody complaining they could barely see the parade. Also, the Borough President was calling a meeting at Borough Hall the following morning to discuss what to do about the smog and wanted the Doctor to attend, and two more people had died in the Sunnyside Section.

Sunnyside Section, the Doctor muttered, hanging up the phone. There was enough irony in that name to choke a cat. When he returned to the kitchen, he asked: "So what was that item on the radio you wanted to tell me about?"

"Seems a truck on its way to Erie hit an oil slick and turned down highway 70. And guess what it was, eh, carrying?"

"What?"

"Ten million bees. The bees got out and motorists were panicking, driving off the road. The Fire Department at Uniontown was called out to hose down the bees. Keep them cool.

Soothe them. Of course, people stranded on the highway were frightened out of their minds. I mean anyone allergic to a bee sting could have gotten killed. What's the world coming to, eh Doc? "

"I don't know. Everything is strange these days, As for Erie, this smog is eerie."

"What's the world coming to, Doc?" Buzz held out the package. "Here's a small package Sandra said she'd take to Bartonwhen she was in New York. You remember? I talked to your wife about some weeks ago."

"Yeah, well, Buzz, there has been a change of plans," the Doctor said,. He turned his face way from Buzz and stared at the cabinet where the dishes and glasses were kept. So many cracked plates.So many chipped cups. When they had been in high school together, he and Buzz had eaten a hundred meals together. What great ambitions they had.

"You mean she's not going? I thought she had gotten tickets to *A Member of the Wedding* and everything. She and her friend Doris. They were going to stay with Barton. I told your wife Barton would help get tickets if there were any problems."

"It's not that Buzz. It's worse than that. "The doctor turned to face his old friend. "Last Sunday night, Sandra was driving home from the movie theater, and she saw a car with its hood up and a man waving at her. So, like a fool, she stopped. You know how Sandra is. Well, when she got out of the car to see what was the matter, she thought she had seen a small child in the back seat, but there was no child in the back seat, just a couple of abandoned beehives, and the man grabbed her from behind, pressed a handkerchief with chloroform on it to her face."

"Oh, my God!" Buzz exclaimed. He staggered back, then fell more than sat, dropping in spite of his thin frame, heavily onto one of the kitchen chairs, allowing the package in his hands to fall to the floor.

"She alive, Doc? Right? She all right?"

"She's alive, but she's not all right."

Buzz shook his head wildly. "No. I guess not." When Buzz was agitated, his slight New England accent returned. He had been born in Maine, spent the first 6 years of his life there, until the family moved to Donora. Buzz's mother had relatives in Donora.

The Doctor put his hand to the stained coffee pot. The coffee was still hot. "Help yourself, Doc." Howard opened a cabinet door and removed a white cup. He found a dish towel and wiped the cup clean. Buzz sat by the table, his body trembling.

"What did he do to her?"

The Doctor rubbed his eyes vigorously. "When Sandra came to, she was blindfolded in a motel room near Webster, tied to the bed. Bound and gagged."

Buzz placed his trembling hands upon his knees and rocked back and forth. "He raped her." He gasped the words out as a combination question and statement.

Doctor Rosemont nodded. He couldn't bring himself to say it.

"That son of a…" But Buzz's religious upbringing prevented him form finishing the thought. "He tied her up and raped her." The Doctor paused and wiped his eyes. For a day and a half, He finally left her in the motel room and the maid, finally able to get in to clean the room discovered her the following morning."

"Tied her up and raped her," Buzz repeated. With his thumb and middle finger, he pressed his eyelids shut.

The doctor removed his gloves, wadded them up and tossed them on the table. He felt foolish wearing gloves inside. He had put them on too soon. Bees made honey; men made tears, and if you were in the midst of tragedies, as who wasn't, tears were a kindness sent by the gods.

"Did she know him? Did she recognize him?"

"No. He wasn't from around here."

"But she can describe him,"

"She can describe him a bit." The doctor paused. Then added, "She won't ever forget him." It was a foolish thing to say.

So many obvious statements sounded foolish until they were repeated over and over, and then the obvious weight of the truth took over.

Buzz felt he couldn't remain seated one more second. He stood up abruptly and paced back and forth in back to the simple wooden chair. Neither he nor the Doc stooped to get the package from the floor.

"I hope they catch him and castrate him. Even that would be too good for him."

The doctor nodded. That certainly would be too good for him. "He had red hair, and Sandra, when she looked in the back seat of the car to see what she thought was a child, saw some bee-keeping equipment. The hat with the protective netting.Some boxes for setting the hives. That's one of the reasons I drove out here though I suppose I shouldn't have left town. I thought you could help."

Buzz sat at the table with his head down. He wept.

"I mean you were once a member of some bee keeping associations," the doctor continued. Did you ever come across a red-haired bee-keeper in this part of the state?"

"Red-Haired bee-keeper?" He did not lift his head. He spoke across his shirt sleeves. "I dunno. That was some time ago. I suppose there must be some."

"At least one."

Buzz brought his head up. Buzz's face was flushed. He was trying to catch his breath as if someone had punched him hard in the stomach. Just the way Houdini died. Some parts of life you just can never get out of. Finally he said very softly, "Funny thing. Isn't it?"

"What?"

"Bees can detect a lot of colors. But not red. To a bee red looks green."

"But he might not be from this state."

"It's possible. Perhaps more than possible"

"I didn't see nothing about it in the paper."

"We're doing the best we can to keep it out of the paper. But someone from the *Independent* will pick it up from the police blotter. I doubt if they are going to care about what my family wants. "

"All my life I wanted to live in a place where I could get a paper on the week-ends," Buzz said, not so much to his friend, but more to himself, said it because it was so difficult for him to find the right words to speak. Finally he added: "But I hear some of those police artists are pretty good. If Sandra can describe him pretty good and they can put a sketch in the paper, there may be someone who'll recognize him."

"And we'll get a hundred calls from crazy people wanting to be a hero or collect a reward."

"You're probably right. Billy and I are out here all by ourselves, so I don't know about people any more. All I know is that strangers scare use. That's why I don't want no new doctor taking care of Billy."

"He kept her blindfolded from the time he

captured her until the time he left."

"I'd kill him."

"Me too," The doctor picked up his black bag. "I'm going back upstairs and look in on Billy. If he's breathing normal, I've got to get back to town. But it you can find me a red-haired bee-keeper in his late-twenties perhaps, early thirties, not much taller than you or me. Empty cigarette packs and wrappers in the waste paper basket tells us he smokes Pell Mells. Eats a lot of Hershey bars. Drinks tea instead of coffee. Drove a blue Dodge. Of course, the car might have been stolen. Might not have been his. The police have been working the stolen car angle, but no one around here has reported a stolen blue dodge. It's obvious there are too many possibilities at this point. The bee-keeping angle may be the best lead."

"I'll make some calls for you and let you know."

"Thanks, Buzz."

The doctor with his black bag went upstairs. On the climb up the well-climbed stairs, he could hear the downstairs phone ringing.

Billy was lying in bed, breathing fine, reading his Bible. As soon as Howard returned to the kitchen, Buzz asked about Billy.

"He'll be fine as long as he doesn't go outside until the smog lifts.Keep the windows tightly shut. And what about you, Buzz? How's the old ticker? Shall I listen to your heart?"

"I'm taking the pills you prescribed," Buzz said. "Don't want another heart attack, though what you told me could bring one on."

"Sorry to burden you."

"Hope I can help you." Buzz reached into the

pocket of his over-alls and brought forth two crumbled five dollar bills. "How much do I owe you, Doc?"

"Forget it, Buzz. Consider it a gift."

"At least take five, Doc."

To keep from embarrassing his old schoolmate, the Doctortook one of the fives.

Buzz picked up the kerosene lamp to accompany the doctor to his car.

"Doc, you should have heard that phone call I just got," Buzz said in the partial darkness, struggling to find something to say.

"Why"

"It was some woman who got the wrong number. When I told her that I wasn't the party she wanted, all she said was, 'Oh, it's all right, I just wanted to tell Rose that her best friend had died. I wanted to reach out to her."

On the return to the house, Buzz muttered to himself, not once, not twice, but over and over, "He had her, he had her, he had her. Even if it was against her will he had her."

The package meant for Sandra to deliver to Buzz's other son remained on the linoleum floor where it had fallen.

II.

"Meet in the center and try it again, hen around rooster, and rooster around hen." The early afternoon square dance at West Bethany had been over for hours, and the people in the church were setting up for a Halloween party for younger members. But Truman couldn't get the call out of his head. *"Meet in the center and try it again, hen around*

rooster, and rooster around hen." Just as he couldn't get out his mind what the Baptist preacher said, that Life was a great gift, but in order for that gift to lead to redemption, it was necessary for each and every person to make peace with himself, with God and the world. Then how easy it would be to step into Eternity.

Truman stared at the gas pump and thought about how he had made his peace with himself and just how much he did not want to make the drive to Donora, but his sixty-two year old aunt was nearly in tears thinking she would miss the baptism of her great niece and the gathering of relatives at the party afterwards. She had brought a gift but was annoyed that her nephew had not cleaned out his car, with the back seat cluttered with his bee-keeping paraphernalia, and newspapers. She refused to place the professionally wrapped gift in the back or in the trunk. She held it in her lap, removed her hat with its veil, placed it carefully upon the gift of a tiny crocheted vest and chattered away.

Truman himself would have bought a gift if he had the time or if he had any idea what to buy an infant. He had no idea what would be an appropriate gift for a brand new girl. His aunt suggested that she buy one in his name, but he had refused. He told her that it just didn't feel right. Not the correct thing to do. Besides his aunt, now dressed in her Sunday best, in her pink skirt with matching jacket, and wear a tango-blouse that Truman's father, many a decade ago, had brought back from Argentina for his sister, had no money. Her way of repaying her nephew was to tell and to retell stories about Truman's father, a man fortunate enough to die in his sleep two days before Pearl Harbor.

"Once at a church softball game with the Mount Pleasant Lutherans, your father was playing outfield, and someone on the other team hit a long fly ball. Your father ran back to get it and he ran right into a large oak tree at the edge of the field. The ball and your father hit the ground at the same time. He was dazed, a bit out breath, but he had that temper you know. He forgot all about picking the ball up. He stood up slowly, turned toward the tree, lowered his head, and ran head on, trying to butt the tree over. He knocked himself unconscious. He had to be carried off the field on a stretcher. Of course, everybody could easily see who he was and what a crazy thing he had done. It makes me wonder if craziness doesn't run in our family. I am, of course, not always in my right mind. But thank God your father was all right, though he never lived that story down."

"See if there is any candy in the glove compartment, will you?"

The difficult driving was giving him a headache.

The aunt opened the glove compartment, and a brooch fell out. There was no candy.

"What's this?" the aunt asked.

Truman glanced quickly at the woman's brooch in his aunt's gloved hand.

"Oh that," he said. "I found that in one of the stores in Webster. I was going to surprise you with it."

"For me?"

"For you."

"Where do you go shopping in Webster?"

"Oh I don't know. Just some store."

The aunt pinned the brooch to her blouse. "Well, I thank you. It's a very nice surprise."

"You're welcome, I'm sure. My father gave you the blouse.I give the decoration. The whole family is involved."

"Every time I look at you, I am reminded of your father."

"Yes, Ma'am," Truman said.

As soon as they entered Donora's City Limits ("Next to Yours, the Best Town in the U.S. A.")—the billboard bearing that greeting could no longer be seen from the highway). Fog and smoke, laden with zinc particles, gathered tightly around the few cars crawling to somewhere else.

"Your father made a great dance team for awhile, not exactly Fred and Adele Astaire, but we did perform for some church groups," the aunt continued, not wanting to talk about the smog because it only made her feel more guilty about asking her nephew make the trip to Donora.

Truman had the sinking feeling that he had missed his turn-off.

"Damn," he said, leaning over his steering wheel trying to see his way through the dust-laden air. Maybe caused by the smelting I plants.

"Of course, all I am now is an old woman. Bad hip. Bad legs, bad eyesight. I'm just an old woman. That's all you need to know about me."

Truman felt a slight reprieve when he saw a set of headlights beaming at him from the opposite lane, though it took him a few moments to realize that the lights were not moving toward him. The car was stopped. As slowly as he was driving, Truman slowed evenmore. He flashed his own lights and blew his horn. He stopped opposite the car and rolled down the windows.

The man in the car could hear woman's voice, but could not make out the words. A man's voice spoke to him, "You all right?"

"Yes," the doctor said. "I just thought I heard a thump under my front tires. Thought I might have hit a dog or something. But when I got out to check, I didn't find anything there."

"That's good."

"Very good. Quite a few dead animals along the highway." The doctor felt terribly tired. If he had his way he would just stay in the car and sleep.

"You sure you're all right?"

"Yes. Thanks. Thanks for asking." The doctor could hear someone talking to him from a car in the opposite lane, but could only make out the faintest of a shape.

"Excuse me, but you wouldn't know where Hill Street would be from here?"

"Off Prospect Avenue. Yeah."

"I been getting in and out the car all afternoon reading street signs. Have I passed it?"

"You passed it. But it's not far."

"We're going to be late for the Christening," the woman said.

"Everything is ten times more difficult in this smog. Look, I'm traveling in that direction. Why don't you just pull in behind me and follow me. I know my way."

The aunt squeezed Truman's arm. "You sure it's not too much trouble?" he said at last, He just wanted to get the afternoon over with. He searched for a pack of Pell Mells in the pocket of his white suit.

"No. No problem at all. Just stick close to the tail-lights. When we get there, I'll honk three times and you take the next right. I'll honk every few minutes to help you keep on track."

"It is mighty nice of you, stranger."

"Don't think twice about it."

"You sure?"

"Sure."

Truman made the turn and waited for the man to get off the shoulder. The doctor drove very slowly, very deliberately. Thecigarette did not taste right to Truman, so he flicked it out the window. He touched the dashboard. There was a fine layer of oily dust on the dashboard.

After twenty or twenty-five minutes of creeping and crawling, a car horn was heard three times. Truman stopped, and as he started into his turn, the car ahead slid ahead until, almost immediately, it could no longer be seen.

"Very nice of him," Aunt Cora said. "Very nice people in Denora."

Truman grunted and studied the houses, looking for a cars parked along the street, he was annoyed at himself, more than annoyed at himself, for missing the street the first time. Smog or no smog, there was no excuse for putting one's self at the mercy of strangers. Cora looked over to her nephew and saw an anger building in him. She said nothing.

III.

By Saturday the smog had gotten even worse, and the doctor was exhausted treating so many sick and

146

panicked people. Thousands of sick people. Old persons coughing up blood were rushed to area hospitals. Firefighters went from house to house dragging heavy oxygen tanks to help restore breathing to the ailing.

Going house to house was exhausting. The firefighters had to feel their way along the wire fences.

To help the sick get to the Charlero-Monessen Hospitals, the Pictairn Fire Department dispatched an ambulance to Donora.

By late Saturday afternoon, after the high school football game, which few of the spectators could see, more deaths had been reported. The doctor's old friend Buzz had been discovered by Billy in his bathroom, dead from a heart attack. At the time Buzz had been fiddling with home-made red dye, trying it on his white hair.. His bewildered son could not explain why.

By early Sunday morning, The Donora Zinc Company and the U.S. Steel and Wire Plant agreed to shut down operations until the smog lifted.

JOURNEY TO DEFEAT RIVER

For centuries everyone knew where Defeat River was. It was in the Waidina Mountains.

Today, should you inquire of a native "Pardon me, could you tell me the way to Defeat River?", you most likely will be greeted with a shrug and embarrassed smile. Sometimes a peasant or an old farmer will point off to the hills and say, "Up there."

Up there. Up.

But where?

2

Jon Suvalick walked away from the Government House. Earlier that morning, he had waited for an elevator with a black woman. The black woman had worn a green beret, a black dress, black shoes. Traces of breadcrumbs from her breakfast remained upon her upper lip. She had been looking for her accountant.

"You looking for the accountant too?"

"No," he said. "A talent agency."

"Oh?" She appeared surprised. "What is your talent?"

"I wish I knew," Jon said. He shrugged. He smiled.

"Well, if you don't know, then who does?" The woman was scolding him, actually scolding him. Her black eyes narrowed.

"I'm a musician," he confessed. The elevator arrived and carried them down. Down. Down.

"What do you play?"

"Clarinet?"

"You playing here?" she asked.

"No. Not yet. But someday you can tell your grandchildren that you rode in an elevator with a famous musician."

The woman straightened. "Now that's more like it," she said. "That's how you should talk. "

When she walked outside into the sunlight, she sang:

E batasatanwize
E mpasituomonanga mu dyambudyakindokie

"You fathers come; we are suffering from witchcraft." Yes, Jon thought that is exactly what we are suffering from.

3

In the old days, one journeyed to Defeat River because the waters were clear and cold and good for drinking. The ritual was simplicity itself.

Arriving at the river, the man, the woman, the child would strip off his or her clothing and leap into the water. The water would clean the body and refresh the spirit. One would arise from the torrents, dress, and returnhome, but now no one knew where the river was, though everyone knew that the waters were miraculous. Defeat River was a great river. If one could only locate it.

Life doesn't really work out the way one expects it to, Jon thought. That was the essential difference between the old and the young: the old knew what it was like to be young, but the young had no idea what it was to be old.

Oh, one could imagine or try to imagine it. One could pretend to know the losses.. Not that Jon himself was all that old. In his early forties, with gray hair, gray moustache. Too old to play Romeo. Not that anyone was asking him to play Romeo. Or Lear. Or anything. The rule of thumb in theater was simple enough: There were very few good older actors around. If you were old and good, you were too successful for small parts. And if you were old and not good, no one really wanted you. And if you were old and hadn't made any headway, you gave up. You went on to other things.

5

In front of the Government House two natives holding fly whisks were talking to themselves, keeping to themselves. When Jon neared them, the man in the red shirt and khaki pants asked: "Don't you get high?"

"No," the other man said.

"Don't you ever get high?"

"No," the other man said.

Jon stared toward the series of hills, purple in the distance, and sighed. One more conversation where words meant one thing to those involved and quite another to the eavesdropper, one who stood under the eaves of a house, listening.

Time to crawl out of life, he thought. Abandon his wife and children, and all the clerical jobs he had undertaken to raise money. Time to go to Defeat River. No sense to wait, he thought, but even he had the good sense to realize what he must do, he would need supplies.

The journey could take several days, weeks even. It would take longer than that if he started out in the wrong direction, if he walked around and around the lower ridges of the mountains, created circles within circles, coming back upon himself.

No, he thought. Tomorrow would be as good a day to start as any. Or the day after. Tomorrow he would purchase a mule and a good compass, find a good map, get enough supplies to see him through for a week or so.

Waiting by the elevator, he saw the old woman in the beret for a second time.

"Did you see Benny Goodman when he visited here?" she asked him.

"No," he said. "I saw him in Manila."

"You didn't see him here?"

"No."

"Then you really missed something." "Yes," Jon sighed. "I really missed something."

6

Jon didn't tell his wife of eight years that he had decided to leave his job at the Government House and that he was going into the mountains. He didn't tell anybody. He merely got the supplies organized. Two women in the supply store had been discussing an old man who had lost his ability to handle money.

"We're just going to have to wait," one woman had said, "until he loses it all, and then we can step in with the lawyers to prove he is incompetent."

"That's a drastic way to do it," her friend said, dragging hundred pound sacks of rice toward her pick-up truck.

"You're telling me! But there's no other way."

About four in the afternoon, Jon set forth.

7

A few miles out of town, Jon passed the remains of the hospital at Limay where he had briefly worked during the war. There had been so many wounded that the Jai-a-lai palace had been converted into a ward. It had been a time when Japanese transports had entered the Gulf and Manila had been declared an open city. The wounded who had suffered from gangrene had been carried to the base of a small hill. The stench. The terrible stench.

The mind could forget many things, but not the smell of things. Smells brought back everything. Of all the pleasant memories of his youth, perhaps the most pleasant were the smells of candy stores with tobacco and new comic books, stack upon stack of them.

A P-40 plane flew over, cast a brief shadow over the land. Tugging at the mule and sweating, Jon remembered the Captain who had shot his horse. His men had gone without food for so long that he did what he had to do.

8

If a person were lost and starving, he or she would eat anything and be grateful. So far, Jon was neither lost nor starving. So far. That evening Jon found a barong-barong and crawled inside. But he did not sleep. It was too hot to sleep.

9

August ended. September began. The children, ages eight and twelve, would be returning to school. The children saying *titser, titser, titser*, for teacher. *Nars* for nurse.

What was the old joke about taking a turn for the nurse?

On the fifth day out, climbing a steep hill and pulling the Mule—whom he know had given the name Gayomard—Jon stumbled and twisted his ankle. Badly.

He lay on the ground and large crabs, known as Alimango, scurried forth to inspect his wound. Where did he come from? And the wonks? He was in a new geography. A geography he had not even considered before. If a stranger had claimed that Jon were lost, Jon would say No. No. He was not lost. He just did not know where he was.

10

A diamond back was killing a rabbit. Jon lay still, his ankle swollen, his tan body covered with sweat, his barong baby soaked though, and listened to the terrible cries of panic.

And the cries died.

He slept. He was back in the Army and dreamt of playing the Clarinet at the Army and Navy clubs. For two years he had worked as a general factotum at the one on the Luneta opposite the Manila Hotel. He redid his tasks. And ended up scalding a live hog in a giant vat. His mother hadbeen born on Scalding Lane and had frequently told him of watching, as a young girl, the hogs being scalded.

He finally awoke to the nuptial song of the Spadefoot toad.

11

Jon realized that he had not planned well, had not brought enough supplies for such a long trip. Had not planned on getting injured, for who plans on getting injured. Only someone very well organized. Had his wife reported him missing? Were the police searching the mangrove swamps for him?

Ya-ow, ya-ow. The cry of the spadefoot toad with its short muzzle and broad head. In the head of toads lurked the Philosopher's Stone. Or so they say. So they say.

The shining green of the mangrove swamp, with the mud infested with newts. The faint odors of gangrene. Why hadn't gone there? Why had he chosen the most arduous way to climb?

"Because you are a stubborn man," a voice said.

"Who's speaking?" Jon had carved a crutch out of a tree-limb and now, with pain, stood up. He must go on.

12

In the course of the night a miracle had happened. Gayomard had become a man. And now he was speaking as if he were an old friend. "I am your friend," Gayomard said. "I have watched you struggle all the way up the sides of the mountains, with the sun burning into your skull, throughthe layers of your skin. Soon you shall be so hungry that you will have to cut out your heart and put it into a frying pan and eat it."

"I know, I know, I know," Jon said, holding his hand over his eyes to shield him from the terrible brightness of being that his fevers had brought on. An entire world hadawakened with him. Startled by Gayomard's new appearance, Jon stepped backward and nearly stumbled into a wishbone bush. I must return to the Government House, he thought. I am going mad. I have worked with themfor a long time. I have done good work for them. They must give me my old job back. An erobomaster spider crawled from the leaves of the Wishbone bush and regarded Jon with its high eye.

"You didn't plan well enough for such a long journey," Gayomard said. "You don't have a food to reach Defeat River."

"I know," Jon said, watching the spider crawl over the boot of his one good foot. "I didn't plan on getting injured."

"It's not fatal," the mule-man said.

"I can't go forward and I can't go backwards," Jon said. He said it matter-of-factly.

"I hereby give you permission to shoot me and skin me and eat me," Gayomard said. "In my old shape, of course."

"Of course. Thank you." Witchcraft he thought. A Griffin vulture floated overhead, glided in the bright blue. The brightest blue Jon had ever seen. The River can't be far from here he thought. But I must rest. I must gather my strength. I cannot reach the River a broken man.

Two days later, after listening to the cries of toads until he felt was going mad, he shot his mule, skinned it, and chopped up the meat, fried it and salted it. Now he had enough provisions to continue. He checked his maps.

The swelling on his ankle had gone down. It was no longer painful to walk.

He would discover the source of Defeat River if it killed him.

13

On the way up the mountain, under a blazing sun, he thought about his wife and how he had met her and why he had married her and how his life had taken its curious bends and twists. (Twist, as in ankle?)

He had met his wife on the streets of Manila. He had been nothing more, nothing less than a street musician. He played classical music and passers-by dropped coins into his opened case. When his wife-to-be strolled by, she looked back. Looking back was no doubt fatal. He spoke toher. They talked. They married. No children. No childrenmade the walking away more possible.

14

The climb toward the source of the river was steep. The sun was unrelenting. His head swam with revelations: We are suffering because of witchcraft. For a time it was two steps forward. Three steps back. The sharp gravel cut into his shins, and, when he fall backward, into his buttocks. His body was a mass of welts and cuts. The tailless whip scorpions taunted him. The three steps forward and two steps back. It was not the animals who were poisoning him. It was the entire landscape with its unnatural blues.

At night he slept in the open, naked to the elements. He ate the final bites of the mule flesh. His teeth ached. His jaw. Two teeth broke and he spat the out. Molars. Teeth eating teeth. He was exhausted. So tired he could hardly move. But, when morning came, he continued his journey. Hesang to keep himself company: *E batasatanwizel E mpasiruomonangamudyambudyakindokie.*

The more he sang, the more he lost track of time. Perhaps Gayomard's witchcraft trick was merely hallucination. There had been food, but the food was gone. The stomach could no longer remember a past feast anybetter than the mind could. His throat was parched.

But there was the river to reach.

15

If he had asked anyone whether he should have undertaken the journey or not, the answer would have been the same, always the same. There is no river in the Waidina Mountains. There are no Waidina Mountains.

Life was merely a strange progression of hallucinations, witchcraft that took a man further and further from himself. At various hours during the day he had been tempted to bend down and pick up the shadows of his world.

The Griffin vulture had found company. Five or six of them now floated overhead. Jon cursed them. "Are you waiting for me to die?" He screamed at them, though his own voice was no longer recognizable.

He looked at his hands, now nearly turned black, and they were covered with blisters. His feet also were blistered and bleeding. In the cool of the evening his body shook with fever and chills. Go back the wishbone bushes cried.

Go back to where?

16

At last it happened.

17

It was late afternoon, when he stumbled forward, and heard the sound of water. The clear cascade of water over rock.Softness over hardness.

Clearness over opacity.

He doubted his own senses. But there it was. He saw it through a line of pine. The river he had been seeking. The water. He crawled forward and more of the river came into view. He let out a shout.

And then another shout. And listened for the echoes. His own voice, harsh and foreign and whispery as it was, returned to him as a warning. There was nothing else in the sky. Even the clear blue sky overhead was a foreigncountry.

He could no longer walk the final hundred yards or so, and so he crawled, with sweat falling from his forehead into his eyes. His hands so stiff he could not open them, his knuckles digging into the gravel and dirt.His entire being in rage. His lips chapped. His head burning.Hisbelly and chest scratched and bleeding.His ankle once again swollen.

There, not far in front of him, was what he had been seeking all the time. He wanted to cry, but he couldn't. There was sweat but no tears. Blood, but no tears.

Rage, but not tears.

What had he wanted to say? He had forgotten.

And the River was deserted. He had it to himself. As he inched toward it, he laughed aloud, thinking of the old Prince of Jakarta who was not able to have intercourse with his wife because fire and flames issued from her vagina.

FIRE

"I do not think it either useful or desirable to interpret as a survival of fire worship the practice once universal in districts where sea-coal came not, of keeping fire constantly aglow on the hearth. Where peat or wood is the staple fuel, burnt on a hearth, not in a grate, no effort is required to ensure the red embers lying overnight, to be fed with fresh fuel in the morning. I have recorded elsewhere a picturesque instance of this occurring on my own property. I took an English friend to fish for trout on a moorland lake. Rain came on; we rowed ashore, and took shelter in the house of the worthy peasant who looked after my boat. As it was past midday, I asked his wife (whose name, curiously enough, was Hester Stanhope) to bake us some scones for luncheon. She complied willingly, went down on her knees, and began blowing away the top of the heap of white ashes on the hearth, thereby disclosing the live red peat below. My English friend was surprised. 'I thought,' said he to the gudewife, 'that fire was out. How long as it been alight?' He told me afterwards that he supposed it has been fresh laid that morning. The gudewife looked up at him from her knees, and said, "It's just seven-and twenty years come marti-mas since Rab an' me cam to the hoose, the fire's never been ootsynce."

"Five-and-twenty years have gone by since those words were spoken. Rab and Hester are both 'in the mools.' The cottage has been improved out of all recognition, and a patent cooking-range has replaced the primitive hearth."

—*Herbert Maxwell in* Notes and Queries. *January 11, 1913.*

I don't know how I get involved with so many social outcasts, but I indeed I am involved. Up to my scrawny neck. My wife—or, my ex-wife, I should say—says it displays lack of character on my part. Lack of taste. Lack of ambition. Lack of—go ahead, you fill in the black. Hester was always fond of starting sentences that began, "The trouble with you is…" or "You lack….." Those sentences would a novel make.

Anyway, for reasons that pertain to autobiography, pubescent Freudians, and a willful desire to self-destruct, I hand around with a bunch of creeps. One of the nicer ones is Joey The Juke Amsterdam. The Juke is a puke of the first water, really, but when he's got money he stands a man to a drink and a meal and a C-note or two to get through the day. And, what with one thing and another, there has been many a day that needs to be gotten through. My brother, unlike my wife—ex-wife I should say—disdains the crowd I hang around with, with the same intensity with which I disdain myself, or at least my own lack of accomplishment in a world that thrives on money and success. He says that's all our lives are: the days we get through. Some of us get through them better than others.

Anyway, I'm going to confess to a day I got through, but which I'm not particularly proud of. My Catholic friends, like the late Philly LaMotta, say that confession is good for the soul. Who am I to doubt them? Who am I to doubt anyone? I have a terrible fear of being burnt alive. I am many things to many people, but I am not Joan of Arc to any of them, except maybe my wife, my ex-wife, who claims I am a martyr to the track. I am the Patron Saint of Out of the Money finishes.

Maybe you remember a few years back a beautiful colt named Sunny Man? It belonged to Mr. Kilmer—

Willis Sharpe Kilmer, to be exact. Well, Sunny Man who ran just fine in the Preakness and the Derby, had been getting up for Havre de Grace where he was the favorite. But somebody, and I can't say who, because I don't really know, slipped him a pill of chloral and arsenic. Some bastard who had more love for money than for horses tucked it into his mouth before the race and there you are. I ahead about two hundred riding on Sunny Jim, but that cold was just plain outrun, beaten by Prince of Bourbon, and everybody knew, especially Sunny Jim's trainer J.P. Smith, something was wrong because the fractions were way off. My fourth grade teacher would laugh. Me and fractions!

After the race, J.P. told the reporters, that he "had worked' him before his race at Havre de Grace. He went the first two furlongs in 22 2/5th seconds, and indicated that he would run six furlongs in close to 1 minute and 11 seconds. In the race he was back in the pack after two furlongs, although it was run by the winner in 23 and 2/5th seconds, a full second slower than Sunny Man worked. Sunny Man finished second, in a race run in 1.12.25, but his race caused me to upbraid the jockey Jimmy Wallace for what I thought was a poor ride."

Losing the race was bad enough, but what happened later was worse. That night the horse went crazy, and Sunny Jim ended up butting himself to death against the wall of his stall. Sunny Jim—whose name no longer applied, banged his head against the stall, smashed his head wide open. Not a pretty sight for anybody, especially for any man, woman, or child who has marveled at the everlasting beauty, call it grace, of a thoroughbred running with four feet off the ground. The world will never be quite that splendid again.

That morning we noticed his mouth was badly burned. His gums had turned green before he died. That's how we knew it was chloral and arsenic. Nobody but nobody should brush his teeth with that stuff.

A lot of people suspected that Joey and a jockey friend of his named La Motta had been involved in the above someway, but nobody could prove it. All you can do in a case like that is take your lumps, put your head down and cry. And I wasn't crying over my lost money. Money you can always get back. Sometimes. I lost every cent I had on a horse named Jiril, but I didn't bear any grudges. But the day Sunny Jim died, I hadn't cried like that since the morning I discovered my wife was in love with another man. Marriages and fixed races. You can't walk away from either of them clean.

I suppose I should have ended my friendship with Joey after that, but as I say, I couldn't prove anything one way or the other, and Joey really had no reputation for fixing races, though it was suspicious that he was always hanging out with Philly LaMotta, but cold decks and hot dice were his specialty. Who's to know? In America, you're innocent until proven guilty. Right? Right. Besides I have more things on my mind that dead horses. I've got to get through the day like everybody else. Still, Mr. Kilmer treated me just fine.

As you may have gathered, in spite of the fact that I have reservations about The Juke, I'm still hanging out with the guy. If I stop hanging out with people I have reservations about, I'm going to end up lonely, and so one morning Joey calls me up to Philly LaMotta's one room digs on Church Street. As I say, Philly LaMotta's a jockey and once a good friend of Jimmy Wallace. I won't comment on the appropriateness of LaMotta's first name, because you know how names are. Parents are always sticking you with a name you'd rather do without. Or a name that's going to sink you in your later choice of a career. You get hit with the wrong name and it ruins your whole life, controls your destiny as it were. My own name is Rob. Rob Barnaby. Call me Barney, I say. My mother hates it how I hang around with gamblers and jockeys and tax accountants. It breaks her heart, but what's a guy going to do if he's named Rob Barnaby? Become a movie star? Not on your tin-type.

So you see, I was ruined before I hardly got out of the womb. Most of us almost are.

My twin brother, Elliott, on the other hand, is a great success. He teaches literature at the Community College. He writes articles for obscure journals and is always cutting things out of magazines and bringing them home. It keeps him from having to talk to us. Anything with our name in it catches his eye. Like, for example, did you know that a Lady bug in England used to be called Bishop Barnaby? Yeah. I didn't know that either, and I could care less, but Elliott collects stuff like that. He and Momma have a scrapbook filled with them:

Mr. Editor, Legour asks why the people in Suffolk call a lady-bird 'Bishop-Barnaby?'

I give the following from the late Major Moor's *Suffolk Words*: 'Bishop-Barnaby. The golden bug. See Barnabee. In Tusser's Ten Unwelcome Guests in the Diary, he enumerates 'the Bishop that burneth (pp. 142. 144), in an ambiguous way, which his commentator does not render at all clear. I never heard of this calumniated insect being an unwelcome guest in the diary; but Bishop-Barney, or Barney, and Barnabee and Bishop-that-burneth, seem, in the absence of explanation, to be nearly related—in sound at any rate. Under Barnabee it will be seen that *burning* has some connection with the history of this pretty insect."

"Barnabee," writes the Major, "the golden-bug, or lady-bird; also Bishop-Barney; which see. This pretty little and very useful insect, is tenderly regarded by our children. One seedling on a child is always sent away with this sad valediction:

> *'Gowden-bug, gowden-bug, fly away home,*
> *Yar house is bahnt down and yar children all gone.'*

To which I add another nursery doggerel:

> *'Bishop, Bishop – Barnabee,*
> *Tell me when your wedding be,*
> *If it be to-morrow day,*
> *Take your wings and fly away.'*

The major adds, 'It is sure to fly off on the third repetition.'

'Burnt down,' continues the Major, 'gives great scope to our country euphonic twang, altogether inexpressible in type; *bahntdeeyown* comes near to it as my skill in orthography will allow.

"Ray, in his *South and East Country* Words, has this:

165

'Bishop, the little spotted beetle, commonly called the lady-cow or lady-bird. I have heard this insect in other places called golden-knop, and doubtless in other countries it hath other names. (E.W. p. 70) Golden-bug is the common Suffolk name."
—*J.G.Southwold. November 16, 1849.*

Read something like that to Joey and he would look at you as if you were queer or something. Not that my brother's queer. He's just different. Give him a pair of scissors, paste, and some old magazines to cut out and he's just fine. My ex-wife likes Elliott just fine too.

Anyway, Joey calls me out of the blue to tell me that Philly LaMotta has got a knife wound in his lung, and he won't go to the hospital because Matella, who heads up the East Side, is going to kill him anyway. Joey wants me to join him at LaMotta's apartment to keep a kind of a death watch. So how am I going to say No to that? Besides, Joey says he has this theory. Dying jockeys, right before they die, always tell you who's going to win the next big race. It's not just a superstition, he says. It's true. All this from a guy who once got himself arrested in connection with a bank robbery after he tried to buy a car with two thousand half-dollars. If you rob a bank shipment of $10,000 worth of half-dollars, you shouldn't try to spend them all in one place. Joey's got balls where his brains should be.

I've know LaMotta (no relation to the boxer) for about seven, eight years. I was there, in fact, the day he broke his cherry. And though LaMotta's no Woodward or Longden, he's a good Italian kid who always gives his horses a good ride. Maybe that's why he's got a knife in his lungs. Sometimes he gives a good ride when he shouldn't.

LaMotta's apartment, if I may describe it to you, is only a room and a half of cardboard walls within spitting distance of the track. There's a livingroom area with a shit-green sofa bed smack in the middle of it, a kitchenette with a coffee pot, a blender, and a couple of hot-plates, and a bathroom with a yellow tub. The place is packed wall to wall with newspapers, racing forms mostly, bits and pieces of yellowed clippings of his glory days (La Motta was named runner-up for the Apprentice of the year), stuff like that.

Because LaMotta was dying, I had the impression the room was more crowded than usual. Too much of the past elbowing and pushing its way in. Under a small trunk was a yellowed paper opened to the story about Sunny Jim. I saw it right away, but I didn't say anything. Why should I? Maybe it was just a coincidence. Life is loaded to bear with coincidence. Like once there was this man in Minnesota who decided to surprise his brother in Sweden and so he hopped on a ship. At the same time, the brother in Sweden decided to visit him. The two never did get together. That's what I mean by coincidence. That's why I would never go visit my brother if I could help it.

There were also a couple of chairs around the sofa-bed, and Joey motioned me over to one.

"Ain't seen you in a long time, Barney," Joey says.

"Same here," I tell him, sitting down next to him to watch the jockey die. It doesn't sound like a lot of fun, but it's something to do.

"Matella suggested I get in touch with you. He says he owes you a favor."

"He did take my wife," I tell him. I take out my handkerchief and hold it out toward LaMotta's face. Joey puts out his hand and grabs me by the wrist. He shakes his head as if to say 'don't waste your time'.

Joey's in his brown suit and tie. Not a bad looking guy actually—slightly less than six feet with a completely bald head waxed to shine. But when he's dressed up, he doesn't like to be nice to people. I don't know why, but that's the way some people are. And his tie is bright green, as if it's St. Patrick's Day, which it's not. It's hardly ever St. Patrick's Day, except for once a year. The tie matches his eyes. I didn't believe people had green eyes before I met Joey. Now he's color-coordinated. He always wears something to match his eyes. He's got a couple of half-dollars in his left hand. He'll never get rid of them.

LaMotta is sprawled across the wet sheets, his mouth hanging open, his forehead bathed in sweat. He's got his jockey whip in his right hand.

"How's he doing?" I asked. I think I should ask something about him. After all, we're in his apartment, if you can call it an apartment, drinking his booze, if you can call it booze. On a small night-stand, there are a couple of candles burning in front of a statue of the Virgin Mary. In the long run he's a better Catholic than he is a jockey. Maybe the odds are better.

"That's how he's doing," Joey says.

LaMotta moans and I pull my hand back and pocket the handkerchief. For the next twenty minutes or so, Joey and I sit in our chairs and don't speak.

I get up, stretch, pour me a couple of fingers of scotch, sit down again. I can't get comfortable. For one thing, the jockey, drowning in his own sweat needs a bath.

For another the room, as small as it is and insulated with newspapers, is cold.

"We need a fire in here," I say.

"We need a fireplace first," LaMotta says. He opens a paper.

"He's never going to get warm."

"I guess it depends which way he's going. Here, hold out your hand."

I hold out my hand. He deposits a half-a-dozen half dollars in them. "Take them. I'm getting tired of lugging them around. They never bring me luck."

"Thanks," I say. "Silver dollars are suppose to bring luck."

"Yeah, well, they weren't shipping silver dollars the day I made my hit."

We waited a little longer. There's not much progress one way or the other. Not only are Italian jockeys few and far between, they're terribly stubborn. Joey reaches into his suit pocket and pulls out a white slip of paper.

"What's this?" I ask. "Christmas?" I open the slip. On it is a number:

80,658,175,170,943,878,571,660,636,856,403,766,975,289 505,440, 883,277,824,000,000,000,000

"That's the number of different ways the cards in a deck can be arranged."

"Yeah?" I fold the slip between my thumb and forefinger. "Is this what Martella's sending me in exchange for Hester?"

"Pretty interesting, huh?"

"Not very," I say.

Joey's face looks crestfallen. I've hurt his feelings. "Maybe your brother would be interested."

"Maybe," I say. "He's interested in a lot of things. You two should get married." I get up and go into the bathroom to look at the yellow tub. It's not very exciting to look at, but it passes the time. I flush the toilet a couple of times. I open the medicine cabinet. Inside there are the usual razor blades and pills, and a paper bag. Being curious, I open the bag. Inside are two small vials. One is marked arsenic. What's a jockey like LaMotta doing with a vial of arsenic? I bring the bag out to Joey.

"What you got? Your lunch?" he asks.

"Look," I tell him, shoving the bag under his nose.

"Giril," LaMotta cries. And then he bolts upright in bed. Christ, it scares the shit out of me. I think I'm seeing something I shouldn't. LaMotta's got his bat and he's whipping the side of his bed into a frenzy. "Giril, Giril, Giril…"

"Jesus, he's out of his mind," I say, leaping up and back, knocking over the chair. "I don't need this."

"Just write down what he says. He knows who's going to win."

"What's he saying?"

"Giril. Something like Giril."

"How do you spell it?"

"How in the hell do I know? I'm not the one with a brother teaching college."

"What about the chemicals in the bag?" I shout at him.

"I don't know anything about it," Joey says. "You think I know anything about that stuff? Ask him." He points toward LaMotta.

"Yeah," I say. "He's in great shape to answer."

"Better than you will be if you don't shut your yap," Joey says. I can tell he's steamed. "You want Matella to be your friend or not?" I guess I brought up a subject I shouldn't.

LaMotta's giving the bed a good ride. He must think he's going somewhere. I wish I had a bet on the bed. He raises his whip, slips between horses, and falls backward. The ride to glory is over.

"What do you think?" I ask Joey. "I think he's still breathing."

"I think he finished out of the money." Joey is leafing wildly through the pages of *The Morning Telegraph*. "Here. There's a horse named *Jiril* running at Monmouth. Here, look." He folds the paper back and shows me. LaMotta's on the bed with his mouth wide open. Martel says to tell you to take whatever cash you can lay your hands on and bet this horse across the board. He says you can't go wrong."

"Who should I thank for this favor? Him or LaMotta?" Joey leans over the bed and pulls the wet sheets up.

I start toward the door. "Wait a minute. I've got one more thing to do." He takes the paper bag from my hand and a can of lighter fluid out of his coat pocket. He gives the bag a good dousing, then grabs a candle from the nightstand, knocking the Virgin off.

"What are you doing?" I ask.

"Don't ask." He flashes me a grin and tosses the candle and the bag onto a pile of newspapers that he has also doused. "Come on, let's get out of here. You got what you need. Nobody needs to look in the bag. Right?"

Five and twenty years have gone by since those words were spoken. And everything has changed. Not necessarily for the better either. We grabbed our hats and beat it, closing the door softly so as not to wake the dead. Running down the stairs, the murder of Sunny Jim, for some reason flashed across my mind. What a shame, I thought. I always felt sorry for Mr. Kilmer. Mr. Kilmer always treated me just fine.

THE LAST HOUSE TOUR IN SAVANNAH

One foot in the grave and the other slipping. If Aunt Cecily said it once she said it one million and two hundred thousand times in her life. One foot in the grave and the other slipping, I suspect it gave her good feelings to say it, for it kept her children and grandchildren and nephews (of whom I am one) and nieces, which at last count totaled fourteen, on their toes. Nobody, but nobody, wanted to lose Aunt Cecily. Nobody that is except for Mrs. J. OgelthorpeMeyerson. Nobody wanted to lose Aunt Cecily.

Mrs. J. OgelthorpeMeyerson, descendant to the Ogelthorpe and wife to a Meyerson, took it upon herself one bright spring to recruit Savannah ladies to escort tourists and sundry other reputable and disreputable visitors through various Savannah mansions and homes. A disreputable visitor, in Mrs. Meyerson's eyes, was anybody who happened to be a Yankee. Of course, nobody ever said Yankee without placing an appropriate adjective in front of it. Georgians do not take the Civil War lightly. It is still simply The War Between the States.

How Mrs. Meyerson ever chose my Aunt Cecily to act as a tour guide is still subject to much dispute. Most likely Aunt Cecily, who was really everybody's Aunt—everybody that is who lived within spitting distance of her wooden frame house across the Colonial Cemetery (my Aunt wanted to keep an eye on the ghosts she said)—was most likely recommended by the Pastor of the Baptist Church, though if you ask the Pastor about it today, he will hotly deny any such thing. After what happened, who is to blame him?

Be things as they may, one fine Saturday afternoon, Aunt Cecily showed up at the Green-Meldrin House and stayed to learn her business. She took to it, as she said, like a duck to water. Perhaps all her years of teaching stood her in good stead. Who is to know why one person is suited to one occupation, and one person is suited to another? I certainly don't because I never had an occupation in my life. However, once my Aunt Cecily got her foot in the door, nothing but nothing could dislodge her. Aunt Cecily lacked some of the finer graces, but she had a lively spirit, a thorough knowledge of Savannah gossip, and so Mrs. J. OgelthorpeMeyerson was loath to create waves. Thus some three years and some ten house tours later, it came as a great shock to my Aunt to be told she was no longer needed. My widowed Aunt was to be replaced by a blond-haired young man who wore a red blazer and who talked as if any minute a tiger was going to leap from one of the Meldrin chandeliers and devour him. The young man in the red jacket was working his way through college and was a relative of Mrs. Meyerson. All in all, it was not a particularly well-thought-out decision. The action was too abrupt for Aunt Cecily's taste, and Aunt Cecily was not a woman used to being treated with kid gloves.

As I look over the newspaper accounts of that incident, I have before me a picture of Aunt Cecily. The photograph in the plain wooden frame is tinted brown and pictures a stern-faced woman of eighty years old, her gray hair tied into a bun, her mouth turned down as if she had bit down too hard on a Sugar Daddy and had broken her teeth. And yes, she still had her teeth at eighty. Our family is famous for its teeth. I could probably make a fortune going on the road with a dental product, but I'm not all that fond of smiling. Few people in our family are.

The photograph shows Aunt Cecily wearing the same plain gray dress with white stripes in it that she always wore, a dress that made her look like a fugitive from a chain gang, and Georgia chain gangs was a subject that my Aunt could wax eloquent upon. You see, Aunt Cecily met my uncles when she chanced upon him lying face-up in a shallow ditch filled with yellow water. My uncle—who was no uncle of mine at that time, because Cecily was all of twenty years old when, as she put it, "Fate jolted her into real life"—was an escapee from the prison and was suffering from malaria. Nobody gave him much hope to live, and so whoever his friends were (and they were no relatives of Mrs. Meyerson, I can tell you that) left him to die. My aunt, who was always a head-strong young woman, so head-strong that my mother lived in constant fear of her, decided not to turn this pathetic creature over to the law, but took it upon herself to drag him to a near-by barn and to nurse him back to health. To make a long story short, Uncle Edgar was eventually caught and returned to prison (Aunt Cecily had her suspicions about the people who turned him in) where he was doing time for passing bad checks—kiting, he called it. It always got a chuckle when kite-flying weather came up. Golly, I swear on a stack of Bibles, that Uncle Edgar could write some of the most beautiful looking checks a body could want. I still have two of them framed on my wall, one of which he used to pay me for mowing six lawns, when I was thirteen years old and madly in love with Cecily's eldest daughter—Virginia.

Golly, what kind of a man would give his own nephew a bad check? It sometimes makes me feel that my family is building a house with an empty attic. Virginia's a school teacher now, so she's not going to like me telling stories about her parents, but my infatuation with her really came to nothing anyway. The same could be said for Uncle Edgar's checks.

Perhaps if Pastor Thomas had told Mrs. Meyerson something of my Aunt's checkered past, Mrs. Meyerson, who lives in grand style within a stone's throw from Telfair Square, would not have considered offering my aunt a job, thus saving a great many persons, myself and my mother among them, acute embarrassment.

In spite of the initial mortification, thought, there are nights I lie awake and think that I would give my eyeteeth to have been a party to Aunt Cecily's final Savannah tour. Perhaps you or one of your relatives or friends were lucky enough to be present. I have heard Aunt Cecily's version, which I'll get to in a moment if you just hold your horses, but I would be interested, most interested in other accounts. You can always write me in care of the Hilton Head Christian Fellowship because there's always someone there to pass the letters along. As I said, I'm not really in love with steady work, but that's my family's fault and not mine. I've got Uncle Edgar's philosophy. I don't take the blame for anything.

Lest you live in Savannah, you may not be intimately aware of the Green-Meldrin House located between Madison and Pulaski Squares in a town that has more gosh-darn squares than any other town I ever heard of, the Green-Meldrin House was built in an eleven-year stretch between 1850 and 1861, built by a cotton merchant named Charles Green at a cost of $93,000. Indeed Mr. Green's house, now considered in all the Chamber of Commerce material to be a healthy example of American Gothic, as my Aunt Cecily might also be so considered, was so highly esteemed during the Civil War—excuse me, ma'am, The War Between the States— that General William Sherman used the house as his headquarters during his occupation of Savannah. Mr. Green attempted to curry General Sherman's favor, but General Sherman was having none of that, but what can you expect of a Northerner whose main joy in life was to burn entire counties to the ground. But, golly, not even that hot-headed Northerner occupied the Green Mansion as well as my Aunt Cecily did when members of Mrs. Meyerson's steering committee dragged her kicking and screaming from room to room, down the stairs, and unceremoniously tossed her right out into the middle of West Macon Street, right into the lap of the law.

"I guess you know, Sonny," Aunt Cecily told me a long time afterwards, calling me Sonny, the way everybody else does, though I don't know why because my God-given name is Castor, named after that lubricating medicine my mother was so fond of administering to each of her eleven children, which I regard as further proof that my entire family plays cards without a full deck, "that on that fateful day there were six Sunday School Teachers, female and unmarried, leastways they didn't have no menfolk with them as near as I could tell, down from Charleston for the weekend, and some college kids from Atlanta, three miscellaneous, and Jasper, Jasper Willpond who was my steady beau then and came on my tours whenever the spirit moved him, and I could see them Sunday School Teachers giving him the once over. Sonny, what you scratching your head for? Your hair planning to fall out like your Daddy's?

"I don't know what my hair is planning to do," I said, annoyed at her criticism.

"I can't tell you, Sonny, how angry I was at being told I couldn't take no more tours through," my Aunt said, pausing to spit out some tobacco, none of which she ever spat none too accurate, which kept her shoes all browned up. She liked the tobacco because it was a comfort to her poor teeth. God knows that nobody in the family could comfort her teeth the way tobacco could. "I was spitting nails. Spitting nails, being taken off the job without so much as how-do-you-do because I had left one of the doors unlocked one night, which anybody might do just once in their life without having the Angel of Death blowing hot air down their back. The only time a body ought to worry about mistakes is when the eraser is all wore out on the pencil. Besides I told Miss Stick-Her-Nose-in-the-Air that I was a guide and not a janitor. A professional guide at that." When Aunt Cecily pronounced the word *professional* she drew out all its syllables to all that its true length implied. She picked up a small piece of pine bark and dropped it for flavoring into the stew that was forever nestled on the front burner of her tiny four burner once-white-but-now-yellow stove. "I did my work like a professional," Aunt Cecily announced, "and don't you ever forget that, Sonny."

I didn't.

"One of those fool teachers from Charleston," my aunt continued, "asked me a fool question about that fool mirror in the living room, and I don't know what came over me, Sonny, but if there was s devil in my heart that late afternoon it was because that bitch put it there, taking my job away from me without-out-so-much- as a how-de-ye-do. So I let my tongue rip. Yes, sir, I did, Sonny. I just followed my tongue from room to room, making up tales that would raise a boil on a peanut.

"I done fixed my best stare into that woman's blotched face, and you know what I said, Sonny? I hope the Lord forgives me but I said they used the mirror to reflect all the lovemaking that went on during orgies." 'Orgies?' the woman asked. "Orgies," I repeated, and kept trying to remember some of the books your uncle used to keep around the house."

"What books?" I asked.

"Hush your mouth. You were much too young to know about such things and I was too religious."

"Hah!" I said.

"Hah yourself. I told that Charleston Sunday School Teacher that Judge Meldrin's parlor was stacked high with naked ladies from morning to night, all of their parts reflected in that great big mirror. Why else would they import such a fine Persian rug? Just for people to wipe their dirty boots upon?

"Of course when I said orgies, Jasper Willpond, who had been standing off to one side with his hands thrust inside his overalls, well his eyes started to flutter like a hawk's. 'What are you talking about, Miss Cecily,' Jasper asked, and I told him I was talking about all the orgies held in the mansion. 'What orgies?' Jasper asked. Hush, I told him. You have no business interrupting me when I'm doing my job. I don't interrupt you when you're unloading manure, do I? 'That's different,' he said. 'It is,'

I said.

"By this time the Sunday School Teachers were standing by the Chinese vase, muttering and whispering to themselves. 'How come you never said nothing about no orgies before? Jasper asked me, and I told him, I said, 'I didn't feel like telling it before now.' Well that old Pastor from St. John's is going to get down on you,' he said. 'Just let him,' I said.

"Now you see that beautiful painting of Christ rising' I told my little group who was now examining every object in the room intently. 'That painting wasn't always here. That painting was brought in specially when the Episcopal Church took over the estate for a Parish House. Before that time, the painting that hung on the wall was about naked women cavorting with the Devil.'"

"You must have had naked women on the brain," I told her.

"Just like every other man in this family," Aunt Cecily said. "And then one of them teachers dropped her jaw down something awful like she was going to bite his head off. 'The Devil?' she asked. 'Why do you think Savannah has so many squares,' I said. 'That's because if the devil's army ever invades, we can run to the cannons and hold him off. But it was something all right,' I told them. "They used to hold secret ceremonies right where you are standing. They used that beautiful marble fireplace over there to burn babies in."

Aunt Cecily stopped her story long enough to pull a plug from her jar of molasses. How she could stand that stuff was beyond me. Still is, matter of fact.

"Babies?" the girl from Atlanta gasped.

By that point, Aunt Cecily had truly warmed to her

subject. "There were quite a few illegitimate children born from all those orgies," Aunt Cecily said. "The highfaluting women certainly weren't going to take the little bastards home with them."

Jasper thrust his freckled hands under the top of his faded overalls. "I don't believe a word of it," he said. "I just don't know what's come over you lately."

"And what's come over you?" my aunt retorted, her hands at her hips and her sharp face thrust up next to his. Jasper shook her head and abandoned the room to my aunt and her band of Sunday School Teachers, some of whom by now were fanning themselves vigorously with their guide books. It sure gets hot in Savannah.

"Yes, sir. They gave birth to those little bastards right on this Persian rug here." My aunt raised her head to catch sight of Mrs. J. OgelthorpeMeyerson.

"Mrs. Joseph, what are you telling these people?" She always referred to Aunt Cecily as Mrs. Joseph. She was the only one who ever did.

Aunt Cecily closed her left eye and cocked her head at a forty-five degree angle. It was an odd habit that she had picked up from her husband, who happened to be a living museum of odd habits. "Just telling them about the orgies," she said.

"Orgies?" Mrs. Meyerson went white around the gills. "Have you gone crazy?"

"No, Ma'am."

"You come with me this instant." She turned back to the door and called for Sarah Everton. Miss Everton, a twenty-eight year old unmarried choir director came running.

"I'm not going anywhere with you," my aunt

announced, and wrapped her arms around the giant Chinese vase. Later she told me, "If they were going to come to get me, Sonny, they were going to have to break the vase to do it."

Mrs. Meyerson turned to the group of tourists, all of whom were standing bunched together for protection. One Charleston matron wearing a purple hat couldn't close her mouth. It stood open like a giant wind tunnel.

"Excuse us, ladies," Mrs. Meyerson announced. "And one gentleman I see, but Miss Sarah Everton here will be showing you the rest of the rooms…Sarah."

"But we like the guide we got," the young man from Atlanta said.

"Of course he does," my aunt said. "He likes to hear the truth straight out. Not how much varnish is put upon the umbrella stand."

"Sarah, will you please take these good people out," Mrs. Meyerson commanded. Sarah Everton tugged nervously at her long white skirt.

"Everybody wants me. What do you want firing me for?" Aunt Cecily shouted, not relinquishing her hold upon the umbrella stand. "Just so your nephew can go to school."

Mrs. Meyerson turned back to my aunt and answered her in the lowest audible speech ever uttered by a human being. "This is not the place nor the time to discuss it." She held out her had toward my aunt, though only God knows why. Aunt Cecily would no more take that woman's hand than she would bake cookies for the devil.

Sarah Everton was doing her best to coax the tour group outside into the tiny garden.

As soon as Mrs. Meyerson's hand touched my aunt's elbow, Aunt Cecily let forth a holler. "You want me to break this vase?" she cried, stopping the tour group dead in its tracks.

"You let go of that vase, Mrs. Meyerson threatened, "or you'll be in jail for the rest of your life."

"It's much nicer outside," Miss Sarah Everton cooed, but the people were having none of it.

"You all just can't stand there," Mrs. Meyerson insisted. "We have a crisis on our hands. A crisis." Mrs. Meyerson could do as much with the word *crisis* as my aunt could with the word *professional.*

Nobody left the room. Sarah Everton stood at the doorway and waved her arms about helplessly. She weighed all of a hundred pounds and looked like a stork standing in a marsh. Mrs. Meyerson bit her lower lip and squeezed her embroidered handkerchief into a tiny ball. At last, the uniformed guard—Arnold Hennessy—the very same guard who had discovered the unlocked door and hand unwittingly planted the seeds of my aunt's fall from race, entered, and without a moment's hesitation, approached my aunt.

"What's the trouble, Aunt Cecily?" he asked. He removed his cap and wiped the sweat from his brow.

Mrs. Meyerson placed her hands on Arnold's shoulders and turned him around. "She's not the one asking for you, Arnold. I am. Mrs. Joseph has been dismissed and won't leave the premises."

"Who's Mrs. Joseph?" Arnold asked, scanning the faces of the Sunday School Teachers.

"Her!" Mrs. Meyerson turned Arnold back to face Aunt Cecily. "Make her leave the premises, Arnold I want her out of this room at once. I don't want her back in this house again. You understand?"

Arnold nodded, but he didn't understand. "What's wrong?" he asked my Aunt Cecily.

Aunt Cecily retreated behind the vase. "No trouble. No trouble at all, Arnold."

"Yeah. Well, I guess I'm imagining all this."

"I was just telling these fine people here how the Governor used to burn babies in the fireplace."

"Draw your gun, Arnold," Mrs. Meyerson commanded, with extreme impatience in her voice.

"No violence! Please? No violence!" the lady in the purple hat pleaded.

"Perhaps you all would like to step outside and see the azaleas," Sarah Everton suggested.

"I can't pull no gun on Aunt Cecily," Arnold protested, twisting his slender body away from Mrs. Meyerson so that she wouldn't take the pistol away from him herself. Though it would not have made that much difference because the pistol was never loaded anyway, at least not since that ill-fated afternoon when Arnold, after shooting a rattlesnake in the back yard, returned the gun to his holster, and accidentally shot himself in his right leg.

"I'm getting the police," Mrs. Meyerson announced. "But don't let that crazy woman get away."

"What crazy woman?"

"Mrs. Joseph. Who do you think we're talking about?"

"You mean Aunt Cecily."

"You let her do any damage to that Chinese vase, and the damages are going to come out of your salary."

184

"I'm only making $.90 an hour."

Mrs. Meyerson was gone. She had rushed off to the downstairs phone. The Charleston Sunday School woman in the purple hat, who had been fanning herself vigorously with a newspaper guide to Sunday worship, collapsed on the chaise lounge.

"You mustn't sit on that," Sarah Everton insisted, and tried to pull the woman back to her feet.

"What's wrong?" Arnold asked my Aunt.

"Nothing," Aunt Cecily told him. "Nothing. For the first time on a long while I'm beginning to think everything is going right."

The college boy from Atlanta tapped Arnold on the shoulder. "Perhaps I could be of some help. I'm a sociology major."

"No," Aunt Cecily insisted. "Now you all just go about your business there with Miss Everton. She'll do just fine."

"Thank you, Aunt Cecily," Sarah said. She tugged at the woman on the chaise lounge, but the woman had fallen backward in a faint. "Oh, my Lord," Sarah exclaimed.

"It's Mildred's heart," her friend said. "She's had palpitations of the heart ever since she was a child."

"Open up her dress."

Sarah Everton stared suspiciously at the young man from Atlanta. "Perhaps you would be good enough to leave the room," she suggested. She turned on her stork-like legs and hurried out for water.

Aunt Cecily closed her left eye and tilted her head toward her left shoulder. "You should go home, Arnold. All this excitement might not be good for your own heart."

Arnold's attention was now directed toward the woman on the lounge. "Get back. Give the poor woman air," Mildred's friend announced. She undid the top three buttons on Mildred's dress.

"I can't go home, Aunt Cecily, I'll lose my job."

"You want to work for Mrs. Meyerson forever"

Arnold lowered his head. There was a long silence between them. At last Arnold said, "I've got a wife and kids at home, Aunt Cecily. You know that."

Aunt Cecily nodded. She did know that.

"And I can't afford to pay for the things you break."

"They can't make you pay for this vase, Arnold."

"But they get lawyers and everything," Arnold wailed. "What do I got? I'm going to be sixty-four years old next month, and I don't have a pot to piss in."

"I thought you were only fifty-five, Arnold."

"I know. That's what I told Mrs. Meyerson."

The woman on the chaise lounge was sitting up by the time Sarah Everton returned with the water.

"For my sake, Aunt Cecily," Arnold said, "won't you come along peacefully?"

Mildred fluttered her long eyelashes and patted her chest. "What happened?"

"Nothing's happened yet," one of the ladies said.

"I can't afford to lose my job," Arnold pleaded. "At my age it's hard to get another one. He shifted his weight uneasily from one foot to another.

"You're all right, Mildred," her friend said. "It just got a little close in here. That's all."

"Please?" Arnold said.

186

Sarah Everton intervened between the two ladies. "Please don't spill any water on the chaise lounge. It's really a very valuable piece."

Aunt Cecily straightened her head. She scratched the back of her neck. In tense situations the back of Aunt Cecily's neck always itched. "All right, Arnold, for your sake. If it were anybody else, I wouldn't do it." She released the Chinese vase from her loose grasp, abandoned her sanctuary for good. As she walked toward the hallway, a few of the Charleston women followed Mildred and Mildred's friend remained seated. "You really shouldn't be sitting there," Sarah Everton mumbled.

Arnold followed Aunt Cecily. There was still a slight limp in his right leg. "Thank you, Aunt Cecily. I won't forget you for this. God won't either because you are doing the right thing."

Aunt Cecily started to hum to herself.

Mildred buttoned the top of her dress. "I want to go back to the model."

"You set right here. I'll call us a cab," her friend said.

"You should have broken that vase. That would have fixed them," I told her. I believed it too. Still do.

"Couldn't." My Aunt Cecily sat down in her tiny kitchen and wiped off her hands on a Woolworth towel. "I couldn't let Arnold lose his job, could I? Of course, he went and lost his job anyway, but that's another story. Some people don't have the sense they is born with." She raised her chin up and began to sing.

You will see your Lord a-coming,
You will see your Lord a-coming,
You will see your Lord a-coming,
While the old churchyards
Hear the band of music,
Hear the band of music,
Hear the band of music…

I couldn't help but join in, could I? Aunt Cecily and I sang that whole afternoon long.

About the Author

Louis Phillips' most recent books are: THE WOMAN WHO WROTE KING LEAR and other stories (Pleasure Boat Studio), THE KILROY SONATA (a poetic sequence) and ROBOT 9 IN WONDERLAND (World Audience Publishers), and FIREWORKS WITH SOME PARTICULAR (stories, poems, plays, & humor pieces, published by Fort Schuyler Press).

Made in the USA
Middletown, DE
07 January 2017